ROB BECKETT
A CLASS ACT

ROB BECKETT
A CLASS ACT

LIFE AS A WORKING-CLASS MAN
IN A MIDDLE-CLASS WORLD

HarperCollins*Publishers*

HarperCollins*Publishers*
1 London Bridge Street
London SE1 9GF

www.harpercollins.co.uk

HarperCollins*Publishers*
1st Floor, Watermarque Building, Ringsend Road
Dublin 4, Ireland

First published by HarperCollins*Publishers* 2021
This edition published 2022

1 3 5 7 9 10 8 6 4 2

Emilia Fox interview from alibi.uktv.co.uk

A catalogue record of this book is
available from the British Library

ISBN 978-0-00-846821-7

Printed and bound in the UK using 100%

renewable electricity at CPI Group (UK) Ltd

This book is for Lou and the girls. If it weren't for you three this book would have been written so much quicker. You really are a drain on resources. In all seriousness, Lou, you are my world and without you and the girls I would have nothing. Long, empty days of nothing. Thank you for growing and delivering our beautiful daughters and for making sure our home is filled with laughter and smiles every day. You're also really fit, which helps. Would now be a good time to ask for a pass to go to Vegas with my mates to watch the boxing? Okay, sure, that's a bit cheeky. How about we settle on a golf trip to Portugal instead? Agreed? Great stuff.

CONTENTS

AUTHOR'S NOTE

Before we start, I would like to say to my family and especially my mum and dad that I love you more than anything. You have been wonderful parents. So please don't be angry about the stories I tell in this book – be thankful for the ones I left out. No one wants to be visiting Dad in Pentonville. The Blackwall Tunnel is a nightmare at the moment.

INTRODUCTION

Fuck me, it's hard writing a book. The stuff I have done in order to put off sitting down to write this is unbelievable. However, the positive I can take from this is that I've absolutely smashed my to-do list. Unload dishwasher – done. Hang up washing – done. Clean hamster cage – done. It's remarkable that I would rather scoop up the shit and piss of a rodent than write a book.

I think it's always hard to write a book, even for people who do it all the time. Authors, I think they're called. I'm sure John Grisham must think to himself, *I can't be arsed to describe what a courtroom looks like any more. There are loads of wood panelling and serious-looking people. Let's crack on.* For me, the difficulty is that every time I start to type a part of my brain tells me I can't.

Rob, you can't do this. You're a stupid little fat kid from a working-class family in South East London.

This is the thought that pops into my head when I attempt most things. I originally believed this crippling self-doubt was part of my personality, down to genes, luck of the draw, whatever you want to call it. However, as time has passed, I've come to think it might be something else. I now believe it's because I was born working class.

As much as we laugh it off, there is a huge class divide in this country, between the varying types of privilege and lack of it. Confidence and opportunity are not a luck-of-the-draw commodity. They are normally inherited or maybe bought from previously successful generations through education and assets. Seeing is believing, and if you have never seen any friends or family members write a book or talk about writing a book, what would make you think it is achievable or even possible? It's not something 'we' do.

Growing up, there were members of my family and friends who didn't read books and, in some cases, couldn't read, full stop. Their grammar was so limited that they would end a sentence by saying the words 'full stop' out loud. That's why it's so important to me to write this book and why I'm so excited about it. I could have hired a ghost writer to do it for me. That process would involve me having a few chats on Zoom with the ghost writer, telling them some stories, and then they would go away and put it down on the page as if I had written it. I wouldn't feel comfortable about that. This is a challenge for me that I want to meet on my own. That way it breaks the chain of being scared and fearful of achieving things in an environment where you're told that you don't belong.

When I hear people talk about legacy and providing for their future generations, for me that's not about acquiring wealth to pass down. I want to set an example to my kids and grandkids that there are no boundaries. If you want to do something or be something, no matter what people say you can do it. If I can help my kids become fearless and full of self-belief that would be my greatest achievement. Passing down a house or money is irrelevant, because if you believe in yourself and you work hard the money comes. However, the money would have really come in handy for me at the start of my career. I'm not saying it would have made me funnier, but if my parents had bought me a flat in central London then I would have been able to do a lot more gigs and not spend about a quarter of my life on the night bus home.

It's not just my brain that has told me I was useless. When I was four, at my first ever primary school parents' evening, my teacher said to my mum, Susan Beckett (aka Big Suze), 'Well, where do we start with Robert? He's never going to be a high-flyer or a high achiever. I suggest you get down to the Early Learning Centre and get some shapes and start him off with them.'

In the teacher's defence, I still don't know what a hexagon is – six or seven sides? Who cares about shapes? Once you've nailed a circle and a square you're pretty much ready for life. I'm far more interested in other things – like exposing mango chutney. Let's face it, people, it's a jam posing as a chutney so it can sell more because chutney sounds healthier than jam. No one would put jam on a curry. There, I said it. I look forward to the legal letters from the mango-chutney association.

Back to parents' evening: hearing a teacher say that you will never be a high-flyer opened deep wounds and created a severe lack of self-confidence. It was a brutal moment in my development that I have never really processed, as it was too upsetting to explore. Even now, as a fully grown adult writing a book, I feel compelled to distract from the bleak information with a comedic observation about mango chutney and my problems with its marketing. I have always used humour to distract from bad news or feelings of sadness and being upset. I was brought up with that approach. All of my family use humour as a coping mechanism. If the world dealt us a shit hand, we would, as a family, make a joke out of it and use laughter as a distraction. *Let's take control of those negative feelings and replace the upset with the joy of laughter.* I don't think using humour to distract is an exclusively working-class tactic, but we are really good at it. When you are working class you get a lot more shit hands dealt your way than the middle and upper classes.

As well as destroying my self-confidence as a child, the harsh parents' evening also ignited a fire inside me. For as long as I can remember I have had a full-on Rocky Balboa chip-on-my-shoulder underdog mentality. I would always think, *I'm going to prove them all wrong*, with no idea how I was going to prove 'them' all wrong and, more importantly, no idea who 'them' exactly were. This lack of academic belief in me from my first teacher must explain why I have made a living out of talking – literally the only thing they don't teach you at school. Even then, I still had to go to speech therapy, as my speech was quite far behind that of my peers. More on that later. Cor, this is turning into quite the story. From simple kid who couldn't speak to sell-out tours and hosting the *Royal Variety Performance*. It's like one of those *Britain's Got Talent* journeys, but without Simon Cowell getting a percentage split from all my work for ever.

Growing up, I didn't know I was working class. I didn't even know that there were different classes. Everyone was like me and my family. I thought everyone was the same. The funny thing about class is that you don't realise what you are until you're put somewhere else and think to yourself, *What the fuck is going on here, then?* That moment for me was the Edinburgh Fringe festival, which is like Hogwarts for actors and comedians and is where I first learned that Oxbridge isn't a place, but two different universities combined. A bit like when Brad Pitt and Angelina Jolie got married and became Brangelina. I learned a lot of other things there too, which I'll talk about later. Another moment when I realised I was working class was when I first tasted craft beer. I have a real thirst for cheap lager in cans. Craft lager makes me feel physically and emotionally sick – £9 a can for a charcoal-butter flavoured hoppy mess?

In the same way that I never realised I was working class, I now fear that I have become middle class but I don't know it yet. It was only when I had kids that it hit me: what class am I now and what class am I going to become? Can you change class? Do you have to apply? Is there a promotion and demotion system? Three trips to the dog track, you're back to working class? On the other hand, if you start dipping carrot batons into red pepper hummus, surely you're going to expect a call-up to the middle-class squad? Or is it like the European Super League: no promotion or demotion, meaning no matter how successful or unsuccessful you become, you are stuck in that league for life?

I absolutely had a working-class upbringing. My wife is middle class. So what will our children be? We are transforming into our own little family. What are we? Before you have kids your career is the big definer of who you are as a person, where you come from and where you are going. It's all ego and promotions, holidays and new clothes to wear to the pub to impress your mates. For me, having kids was when I really started to understand who I was and who I wanted to be. Whether you have an influence on that is another matter. So that's why, at the age of 35, I've found myself with the urge to write a book about class. It's been a confusing few years and I hope by getting my thoughts down I might begin to make some sense of it all. Hopefully, by the end of the book we will have worked out what class I am, at least. Then we can make a decision whether or not to fully embrace the answer. Whether it's working class and I only drink Stella in my local pub in Bromley, or I go full middle class and buy some red corduroys and move to Gloucestershire, only time will tell.

Before we begin here are some things you need to know about my current home life: I am married to my incredible wife Lou. When I say she's incredible I mean that I find it incredible that she will just pile up cardboard boxes by the back door and expect them to be put in the recycling bin without a word being said. Incredibly they always are. Lou is a history teacher with a master's degree and is born and bred middle class. She had never eaten fried chicken until she met me. What a lucky lady. Lou, meet the Colonel. Colonel, meet Lou.

Lou isn't just a bit middle class – she is painfully middle class. When we got married she went for the double-barrelled option. Her married name is now Louise John-Lewis. However, in line with her current spending habits she may need to change that by deed poll to Louise White-Company, which, unfortunately for her, sounds a bit like a racist political party. She squeezed out our two outrageously cute but devastatingly exhausting daughters Malcolm, aged five, and Gavin, aged three. They were born middle class – immediately cradled in John Lewis blankets on arrival into this world. I, at 35, have still not felt a Johnny Lew-Lew blanket upon my skin because that blanket is 'for show' in the front room.

So not only do I need to work out what class I am, I also need to find out what class they are. As a family do we all need to be one class? Or could we all be different classes living in one house? My daughters already correct me on my pronunciation of the word 'water'. I currently pronounce it 'waltarh', much to their amusement. 'Daddy you talk funny,' they will squeal with delight in the back of the car as I silently seethe and drive my daughters around like an unpaid private taxi driver that they openly mock. It's weird to be a working-class man who is actively breeding middle-class people. But am I a working-class man or a middle-class man in denial sitting in his Nissan Qashqai with a roof box en route to Center Parcs?

Malcolm and Gavin are not their real names. I keep that quiet in case I go on *Strictly* and have an affair. It enables them to keep a low profile in the eventual media storm. Their arrival in this world made me question everything. Until they came along, I was just a commoner chancing his arm in the world of comedy and TV, looking at it like a smash-and-grab job: 'Let's see how well I can do before they realise I'm just a little oik robbing a living.' Waiting for the tap on the shoulder from the mafia don of TV, who in my mind is David Attenborough, to tell me, 'Enough is enough, Bobby, son, off you go back to the flower market,' then some stuff about plastic in the ocean and saving the whales. Once the girls arrived, I realised that I wasn't just one bloke on a mad adventure. I have responsibilities now, not just financial but psychological and behavioural. I want to be the best dad and husband I can.

So we had the girls and then the big compare happened. Every major life event that came along for my kids made me think back to my childhood. First word, nappies, holidays – it was all totally different to my upbringing. Everything I did felt wrong. It was too working class for my wife and her family, but it was too middle class for my family. I'm always trapped in between. My biggest worry is that if my children grow up with a completely different childhood to mine how will I bond with and relate to them? Will I resent their privilege that they have had no control over? They were eating avocados on toast as babies – I didn't eat an avocado until I was 31. Hopefully this book can help me examine my upbringing and theirs so I can find similarities and not become a lonely old dad, with kids living in Australia, as far away from me as possible.

I've always felt slightly trapped between the two camps of middle and working class. I remember one weekend, going to the pub on a Friday for a few pints with old mates after work, and I was the only one not in high-vis clothing. Then, on the Saturday, I was invited to lunch at Annabel's, a members' club in Mayfair. Sitting to the left of me was James Middleton, brother of Kate Middleton. Literally the brother of a princess. To my right was a businessman who was in charge of launching Uber in Russia. The range of conversations I had that weekend was incredible. From pints to princesses to Putin in 24 hours. All I could think was that my black-cab-driving dad was going to be fuming about me having lunch with this Uber bloke. When I go to the pub with my mates from school who are gas fitters I'm the la-di-da media luvvie and they rinse the piss out of me. Then at work, on a TV show, I'm the cockney-geezer lad. That was fine when it was just me – I could deal with it. But now it's not just me. There are two little girls looking at me, asking questions I can't answer: 'Daddy, why is the gravy on your pie green? Daddy, why does your voice change when you speak to different people? Daddy, why is Mummy crying when you dance with the lady on *Strictly*?'

This book is not an autobiography, but there will be some cracking name drops, don't you worry. I've got to get some press for it somehow and I'm too tired to have an affair or sex scandal. Later on, there is a great story about the time comedy legend and head of vegans Romesh Ranganathan was so angry during a show in Windsor that he headbutted a swan. But he didn't eat it. Always a vegan, even in rage. I mean, I've just made that up, but I can't imagine Romesh would sue me. Or would he? Either way it will be great press. Can you imagine that *Judge Romesh* episode?

I'm hoping this book will help me understand the life I've lived and the man I've become, so I'll be in the best possible place to help my children navigate their lives. I want to make sure we have a long and healthy relationship. Hopefully when you read this book you will find that you have similar stories and feelings and we can all connect together. Maybe you're standing in the book aisle of a supermarket with two screaming kids, trying to put off the big shop and having a similar crisis to mine. Reading this might help you out. Or maybe you're a fully fledged toff reading this in Waterstones after nipping into Fortnum & Mason for a four-quid loaf of sourdough and you want to see how the other half live? Or you're three pints into a stag do at Luton Airport at 6 a.m. and you've ducked out of the pub to look at the books in WH Smith and you're thinking, *I really want to buy this book because Rob's a bit like me. But if I buy a book on a stag do all my old school mates are going to call me 'book wanker' for the rest of the weekend and potentially the rest of my life.*

Whoever you are and whatever your background, you are going to get something out of this book, even if it's just a load of laughs. You can't put a price on laughter, can you? Actually, you definitely can – about 15 to 20 quid this book retails at. Personally, I think that's a bargain. I'm not writing this book to prove a point to anyone. It's just something I have wanted to write about for a long time. I've got no ego to stroke, no scores to settle or points to prove. But actually, thinking about it, that prick teacher at the parents' evening could really do with some points being proved right in front of their fucking face.

I have split the book up into chapters that look at the different aspects of my life growing up and how I experienced and viewed them as a kid compared to now, as well as what my kids have experienced. We will look at birthdays, holidays, confidence, education and all sorts. I don't know about you, but I think giving the chapters numbers is so boring. Also, if you're not feeling the Education chapter you can bin it off and move straight onto the Christmas chapter and it all still makes sense. Cos let's face it, we don't always read the books we buy, do we? Plus, you might just be in a festive mood that day. You're in a mulled wine mindset? Jump straight to Christmas. Personally, I'm mulled wine over mulled cider. I tried it last year and it was quite a traumatising experience. It's like someone just put Strongbow in a kettle. It tasted like boiled piss.

Thank you for buying this and I appreciate you reading this far, but if you stop now there are no hard feelings. But if you're in the shop reading this intro and deciding whether to buy it or not, please just buy it. It's taken me fucking ages to do this. I can see why retired footballers just get a ghost writer in now.

I should probably quickly introduce you to a few other characters that will appear in the book. I have four brothers, Russ, Darren, Dan and Joe. My mother is known as Big Suze, the matriarch and boss of the family – incredibly loving and kind but will not take any bullshit. My dad is Super Dave, one of the most affectionate and loving parents you could wish for. He is also what can best be described as 'silly as arseholes'. A phrase that doesn't get used enough.

This is a good bit of info on my dad: he didn't read a book until he was 43. Forty-three is very old, isn't it? In his defence he didn't get much of an education, as he is dyslexic, and he left school at 13 and became a van driver. At the age of 13 he was driving a van – the good old days when children would drive vans instead of joining gangs. My mum gave my dad *The Secret Diary of Adrian Mole, Aged 13¾* to read, as it was an easy book for a first time. Plus, as it was written as a diary with daily entries, it wouldn't be overwhelming and he could read it in little chunks when he was waiting at taxi ranks for a fare. Isn't that the sweetest story ever? Adrian Mole opened up my dad's world and he now reads all the time. Thankfully he has moved on from children's diaries. It's not a great look for a 77-year-old man to be reading a kid's innermost thoughts.

So, after not reading a book until he was 43, now his son is writing his first book at the age of 35. (That's right, *first* book – there are going to be more; even though I was nervous I have loved writing this.) EXPLOSIONS! FIREWORKS! MUSIC! CHEERING! Cue brain: *Rob, you can't do this. You're a stupid little fat kid from a working-class family in South East London.* Shut up, brain. Yes, I can do this – I'm going to prove *them* wrong. I've never been more focused in my life to write this book. I hope you enjoy it as much as I have enjoyed working on it. Roll on, Chapter 1. Shit, I'm not numbering them. Roll on, The Working-class Test.

THE WORKING-
CLASS TEST

Before we kick off this journey of self-discovery, I think it's only fair that I quickly prove my working-class credentials. I know what you are thinking: *Is he the real deal or is he secretly a middle-class bloke pretending to be working class in order to have a career in comedy?* No, of course not. That's Lee Nelson's schtick.

So who am I? I grew up in South East London and my dad was a van driver, then an oil-tanker driver and he finished off his career as a London black-cab driver. How blue do you want my old man's collar? My mum stayed at home to look after the kids, and when we were older got part-time work in a shop and then worked at a college in the library. I started work at 14 on Columbia Road flower market and did a series of low-paid jobs before I became a comedian. These included bar man, waiter, office temp, cricket steward, shelf stacker and car-boot sale entrepreneur.

I gave up on boot sales when I watched my mum sell a bag full of my Microstars football figures for about three quid. I have never forgiven her and occasionally, if I'm feeling a bit too happy, I will search for my old figures on eBay to see how much they are worth now to bring my mood down.

For my sixteenth birthday I had my party at Crayford dog-racing track, where I openly bet. There were a number of tables next to a window looking out over the track, where we ate and drank and bet on the dog racing. Imagine Ladies' Day at Ascot done on a really low budget with no dress code. All my family were there: aunties, uncles and cousins. It wasn't done in an ironic hipster way – we all loved it. Only looking back now does it seem an odd place to go for a sixteenth birthday party.

My family aren't massive gamblers but will have the occasional bet on the football on a Saturday. When I was young we would all get an accumulator and watch the goals go in with Jeff Stelling on Sky Sports. That's how we would spend our weekends. My wife had no idea what an accumulator was. The first time she ever went to a bookies was when we went to visit my parents on a Saturday. Around lunchtime we, as a family, all set off to place our bets. It was remarkable watching someone experience a bookies for the first time. She was so confused by everything – the clientele, the betting procedure, the odds system – which is totally understandable. I have been placing bets for years but I still get a bit scared and overwhelmed when I hear someone put £100 on a computer horse race at 7/2. Other things that I have introduced to my wife include pie mash, fried chicken and pegging. Not all class related, but still educational.

Grandad Sid was a milkman and Grandad George was a bingo caller, and we had jellied eels at his funeral. Surely that's enough proof that I'm qualified to write this book. What more do you need? I'm writing this dressed as a Pearly Queen and I've just said, 'Cor blimey, guv'nor,' out loud. Right, where's my working-class membership card?

CHRISTMAS

Things I did before I started writing this chapter

....

TWO COFFEES

....

SHOWERED AND FULLY DRESSED

....

BREAKFAST FOR ALL THE FAMILY

....

**CONTEMPLATED BREAKING DOWN
CARBOARD FOR RECYCLING BUT
IT WAS TOO COLD**

....

When it comes to family, class and traditions, Christmas is the great leveller. I loved Christmas so much as a kid. It was easily the best time of the year without doubt, but it was competitive in our house. My two eldest brothers, Russ and Darren, were much older than the rest of us and a product of my dad's first marriage. Technically they are half-brothers, but we have always just ignored that and I would feel quite challenged when people commented on it.

'So, they are your half-brothers?'

'No, we are all just brothers. No half, no full – just brothers.'

I think now the term is a blended family, but that didn't exist when we were kids. There were just fucking loads of us. The term in the 1990s was a broken home, which sounds so bleak. Growing up, a lot of my friends came from what the media would call a broken home. However, it never felt broken to us; it just felt like lots of people who loved each other all in a house. Sure, not everyone looked like everyone else, and if you cut us open and examined our blood and DNA it wouldn't match, but who cares at that point? I would be far more worried about the lunatic breaking into the house and cutting us all up to check our DNA. Leave it out, mate, it's Christmas.

From as early as I can remember, Russ and Darren would always come over on Boxing Day to do presents and eat. Eating is an Olympic sport in Casa del Beckett, especially at Christmas.

So, Christmas morning would be me, my older brother Dan and my younger brother Joe. I was in the middle, which explains a lot. I would wake up first, normally about 4 a.m., which according to my sleep-deprived mum was 30 minutes earlier than normal. My mum reckons I woke up at 4.30 a.m. every day for five years. I always thought she was talking bollocks until I had children. My kids love a 5 a.m. start. It's brutal. It's just in my genetics: I'm an overactive, over-energised relentless lunatic and so are my offspring. Me and my kids ... and before you start, I'm fully aware that to be grammatically correct it should be 'My kids and I'; however, you *know* what I mean, and this is how normal people speak. So deal with it. So, *me* and my kids need about five hours' sleep a night to function the next day. Only five hours. Lou's womb is like a Margaret Thatcher robot factory. We cannot breed a sleeper. I told Big Suze how tired I was and how hard it was and she laughed in my face. Cackled so loud I actually stepped back away from the howl. Then, disturbingly, I witnessed this surge of excitement and energy in her eyes that I can only describe as cold-blooded revenge. She had no sympathy at all. She just laughed and said, 'How do you like it now? I did that for five years on my own when your dad was away long-distance lorry driving and staying in hotels.'

At 4 a.m. on Christmas morning I was sent back to bed, as it was 'too early'. So, I lay in my bed staring at the ceiling, thinking of ways I could wake my brother up without being seen to intentionally wake him up. We shared a bedroom so I would fluff up my pillow really loudly, yawn really loudly, drink my bedside water really loudly, hoping he would stir so I could say, 'Oh, are you awake too? It's Christmas! Shall we see if he's been?' Once I had woken everyone up, we would run downstairs to see if he had been. We didn't really do stockings, just a big bastard sack of presents in the front room.

Before we opened the presents, we would go to see if Santa had eaten a mince pie, drank some beer and given Rudolph his carrot. We would check the front doorstep, where we left it all. That's right, the front doorstep. I didn't know that was weird until I was 32. Me and Lou had all the bits to lay out for Santa that Christmas: mince pie, carrot and sherry, not beer. I was too consumed with rage about the sherry instead of beer to notice that Lou was taking the Santa treats to the front room, with our first child, who was a toddler then, in tow. Christmas traditions are a sacred thing for a family, so when you start a family of your own you enter a Brexit-level set of negotiations with your partner about what traditions your new family will adopt and discard. So far, I had lost the beer vs sherry battle. Little did I know, I was about to lose the war too. Lou entered the front room and laid the treats down.

'What are you doing, Lou?' I said. 'Santa treats go on the front doorstep.'

Lou looked at me like I had escaped from an asylum. The problem with being a comedian is that people think you are always messing about and being silly. No one ever takes you seriously. Which is normally fine because I don't take much seriously apart from things like Christmas.

'What are you talking about, Rob?' Lou asked.

You need to bear in mind that there was a child who still believed listening to everything we were saying about Santa, so we needed to tread carefully.

'The front doorstep, Lou,' I said. 'You put the treats out on the front doorstep and you check them in the morning. That's what we did as kids. Father Christmas has his pie and drink then comes through the front door, puts the presents under the tree then leaves. How else is he going to get in the house, Lou? Think about it.' I smugly chuckled to myself while tapping the side of my head at Lou. 'Come on, brainbox, how is he getting in?' I arrogantly slung in an 'isn't Mummy silly' eyeroll at my toddler.

Lou was still looking at me in disbelief, until my barely able to properly speak child pointed and said, 'Santa chimney, Daddy.'

Yep, that's right, I didn't know that Santa came down a chimney at 32. I'll be honest, I didn't even really know that I had a chimney in my fucking house in the first place. I was learning a lot in one moment. My new chimney, which had been brought to my attention by a child still in nappies, had no fireplace surround to it. When we moved in, I just thought it was a weird hole in the wall where Lou kept decorative logs for no reason. Don't get me wrong, I'm not saying I don't know what a chimney is – let's be honest, a hundred years ago I would have been sweeping them – but we never had a fireplace growing up so it had never occurred to me that Santa might come down it. Also, this is a man who can bend the space-time continuum to deliver presents. Surely he can pick the lock of a cheap front door left on a Yale latch lock most of the time. Let's face it, I love Father Christmas but there's no getting away from the fact that he's a big fatty fatty boom boom. Surely the front door is easier than a chimney.

I was so conditioned by years of walking to the front door that I just thought it was what you did. It's stuff that you don't question as a kid that you can believe for ever. If you never go anywhere new or experience different cultures or classes, why would you question it? My mum once told me that Jeremy Beadle, a TV hero of mine growing up, had a small hand because he played with fireworks, in an attempt to stop me playing with fireworks. I believed this for 30 years until I googled it and found out it was because of Poland syndrome and not a Catherine wheel injury.

I had to concede that yes, it made more sense to leave the treats by the chimney, and that's what we do now. That's our tradition. This may sound sad but once Lou and the kids are in bed on Christmas Eve I still pop out a mince pie, beer and carrot combo on the doorstep for the big man just in case he fancies a walk through the front door for old times' sake.

In order to cope with the changing Beckett Christmas traditions in my house, I have introduced a new family game called Yorkshire Pudding Catch. To play, I stand against the wall and my daughters are allowed to throw the leftover Yorkshire puddings at me as hard as they can. Once I catch one the game is over, but until then I am getting smashed to pieces by pudding. My daughters found this game absolutely hilarious. Obviously throwing food is bad, but at Christmas they are allowed a special treat. Even Lou got involved and threw a slightly burnt pudding so hard at me it actually left a mark.

This game is all fun now, with my children being three and five, but my concern is that as time goes by and they get married and have kids, there is a real possibility that I will be an 80-year-old grandad facing a Yorkshire pudding firing squad because of 'tradition'. I will be sitting in a wheelchair with the brake on, getting mercilessly pelted by Yorkshire puddings. Too weak to catch any, I will just sit there being massacred until the Yorkshire puddings disintegrate on my frail skin. If anyone reading this is judging me for the food wastage, let me explain. We had around 25 extra Yorkshire puddings left over because it was the cancelled Covid Christmas of 2020. I had ordered food for 15 people, as we were due to host Christmas at our house until Boris made dinner with your family illegal a week before. I've still got a pavlova and three tubs of turkey gravy in my freezer.

Back to the 1990s and the present piles: we would take turns opening presents one by one. This is a polite way to do it but a high-risk gamble from my parents because you need to make sure that each kid has an equal number of presents to avoid conflict. One year I felt very hard done by and I wouldn't let it lie. Joe had an extra present. Not any old extra present, but a bright orange Bosch mobile phone. A pay-as-you-go phone from the early days when if you didn't have credit on your phone it wouldn't accept incoming calls. What a brutal way to live. It was also WAP enabled. Before WAP was a filthy sex song, it was text-based internet in the palm of a 13-year-old child's hand. The internet was a new and exciting world. A kid at school had a 56k dial-up internet connection at home that his dad needed for work. The first thing we asked him to do for the lads at school? 'Can you print us off some porn and bring it in? We will buy you ink.' How old does that make me look? PRINT ME OFF SOME PORN! That's what we thought the internet was going to be. Every home would become an indie pornographic print house.

So, let's break down the presents at this stage. Dan, who is six years older than me, is out of the sibling rivalry age. He's earning his own money doing a Saturday job and wants cash and designer clothes for Crimbo. Me, 13, and Joe, 11, are at our competitive peak, and he has one extra present. I am not being ungrateful, I had a great year: some VHS tapes, albums, football kit and the big present, a Matsui TV and VCR combi. *Oh my God, I've hit the jackpot!* I was truly blessed that year. Joe got all the same as me but his big present was a Sega Dreamcast. *Holy FUCKING shit sticks! What a year. We share a room and we've got the Dreamcast and the TV combi!*

I was loving life, but Joe's extra present of a mobile phone still gnawed away at me. So I asked my mum why Joe got the extra present. The stock but normally impenetrable response from my mum was, 'It's completely fair and even. I spent the same amount of money on all of you.'

That wasn't enough for me. I couldn't leave it. I needed more answers so I went to work with a calculator, a shandy Panda Pops and the Argos catalogue. I added it all up and made a breakthrough. I felt a tingle of accomplishment and anger through my hands, arms, spine then eyes, like a police detective finding the piece of evidence to catch a killer. I marched off to the local judge to get a warrant. In reality I walked two steps from the table to the kitchen and presented the evidence to my mum, who was trying to cook 500 potatoes in a red-hot oven. She shut the oven door and turned to me with limited vision as the heat from the oven had steamed up her glasses.

'Mother, there is something you need to know: you are a liar,' I said. 'I have added up the cost of all the presents and Joe had £85 more spent on him than me. I rest my case.'

Big Suze used her stock response: 'It's completely fair and even. I spent the same amount of money on all of you.' She attempted to move more potatoes; the steam on her glasses grew thicker.

I moved forward and pushed my Argos catalogue calculations in front of her blind eyes. As I did this some potato fat spat at her and she yelped. I wouldn't let it go. In a sterner voice she repeated, 'It's completely fair and even. I spent the same amount of money on all of you.'

'No, you didn't!' I yelled back. It's all very Kat Slater in *EastEnders* at this point.

'Yes, I did!' my mum shouted, juggling red-hot potatoes in what felt like the opening scene to *Casualty*.

'No, you didn't!' I shout.

'FINE!' she replied. 'You wanna know the truth?'

'Yes, I do.'

'The phone was nicked – that's why it was cheaper. Okay? Someone nicked it from a warehouse and sold it to us. Happy now? So, as I said, it's completely fair and even. I spent the same amount of money on all of you.' To be fair, she was telling the truth to a certain degree.

Now, I should mention theft and stolen goods. I don't dabble in that world myself, but growing up in a working-class environment it happens and there are certain rules. For example, no one in my family knew or associated with anyone who would burgle houses or steal from people. That was a no-no and quite rightly treated with real disgust and hatred. Invading someone's personal space and home, especially if children are in the house, is a horrific thing to do.

I have been burgled and it's absolutely awful. It happened to us before we had kids, thankfully. What a weird thing to be thankful about. Thank you for your kind consideration, Mr Burglar. I was in the middle of a tour and was finding being away on my own tough, so Lou came with me overnight to Stratford-upon-Avon. We got home around midnight and the back door was smashed in. We phoned the police and Lou's parents came over to pick her up. She was heavily pregnant at the time and obviously very upset about the break-in. They took her home and I waited in an empty burgled house for the police, absolutely petrified. Sitting in the freezing cold with the door broken and wide open, I hoped the burglar wouldn't come back for my Panini sticker albums that were more expensive than the fake Spanish market Rolex he'd stolen.

The police arrived and I felt safer. They took a statement and then they left me there with the forensics officer. This was about 2 a.m. and the forensics man was nearly finished. I didn't want him to finish. I had to stay there until the morning because the back door was wide open and the door-fixing people weren't coming until the next day. I wanted the forensics man to stay with me to keep me safe, so I did two things that I regret.

First of all, I said to him, 'When you've finished dusting for fingerprints do you fancy a cup of tea or a beer?' He declined the offer. A real hammer blow. I felt pathetic, like a lonely Alan Partridge trying to make friends with the Travel Tavern staff. Secondly, I did something really naughty. I hid the forensic man's fingerprint powder tub. My thought process was that if I hid the powder, he couldn't leave me on my own, as he would have to find it before he left. I could drag it out until daylight when all the monsters and burglars went to sleep. So now in one evening I had been the victim of a burglary and also been guilty of stealing forensic equipment from the police. Unfortunately he didn't give a shit about the powder and he left me to sit alone in the freezing cold, staring at the empty space where the telly used to be.

So certain criminality like burglary, drugs and violence is totally unacceptable and is judged and rejected by the working classes, just as it is by society in general. But there are certain criminal acts that are accepted in the working classes – far more gentle crimes and bending of the rules. When I was a kid there was a thing called being 'on the fiddle'. This was the socially acceptable form of theft, where you would be working for a large company or corporation that earned millions of pounds, so if you took a couple of things from the warehouse – an orange Bosch phone, for example – it didn't do much harm. It was seen as an unofficial employee benefit, a victimless crime. I don't agree with it and have never done it, but it did happen a fair bit growing up. I've been at barbecues in South East London and people would turn up with actual McDonald's patties to cook on the griddle. One of my dad's mates fiddled so many books from his van when he was a delivery driver that he had his own book stall on Woolwich Market due to excess stock.

Growing up, these stories were told by my older family members and romanticised to some extent as Robin Hood-type deeds – robbing the rich to feed the poor. It was a moral decision based on how much their family needed something compared with how much the company would miss that item, or in some cases even notice that it had gone. People would brazenly brag about the fiddles they had on the go. I remember one of the jokes I would hear growing up, 'Me and the wife work in the steel and iron business. I steal and she irons,' which is a pretty good joke, to be fair, if a little sexist for 2021. I've heard that joke from about 15 different people, which shows you that even jokes get nicked in South East London.

Looking back, I think all of the talk of the fiddles people had on the go didn't excite me – it just made me worried that the police were going to 'get us'. I'm not even sure what I mean by 'get us', as my family were never directly involved in this fiddling. But we were surrounded by people who were. I look back and judge it slightly, but was this fiddling done for the fun of it or was it done out of necessity? Sometimes the laughing and joking in working-class families was used to cover up the worries and guilt about what was going on. The pressure to provide money to put food on the table and get your kids presents at Christmas can be too much. Imagine it being Christmas Eve and you have worked hard and honestly all year, but you can't afford presents for your children or a turkey for dinner. Then someone offers you a half-price turkey, no questions asked? Rightly or wrongly, people do what they have to do to provide for their family when times are hard.

This section of the book was due to end here but my publisher said it finished too abruptly. Which it did, to be honest, and the reason for that is that I find it very difficult to talk about this stuff in a book, as it's hard to know how much to reveal. I want to be as honest as possible but I also don't want friends and family to be arrested – and I don't want to be seen to be grassing people up in a book. It's muggy.

Radio silence was an essential tool growing up in South East London, as the worst thing you could be was a grass. Even at primary school, it was thrown about as an insult to anyone who would grass someone up to the teacher.

I was brought up with mantras like 'never speak to the police, don't even give them your name, as they can't be trusted' and 'never hit first but if someone hits you make sure you hit them back'. When my children complain about the behaviour of another pupil at their school, my wife says, 'Make sure you tell the teacher.' I know that's the right thing to do but part of my brain is thinking, *What are we doing here, raising a couple of little scumbag snitches? Not on my watch. Ignore your mother. If someone hits you, hit them back and keep hitting them until they go down. Then you can back off.* I think I'm going to find a middle ground and take them to a boxing gym so they can learn to fight and people leave them alone out of fear. That way, they never actually have to knock someone's block off.

This chapter was supposed to be about Christmas but it's turned into the chapter about stolen goods and children fighting. But isn't that what Christmas is all about? Well, in our family it was. Me and my brother Joe used to have boxing matches in the front room and my dad would referee and the family would watch. We had gloves so it was fairly safe – it wasn't a bare-knuckle straightener. However, there were no headguards so we would buzz each other a bit with a solid jab. I was about eight and Joe was six, which might sound unfair but Joe was fucking massive for his age. If anything he had the height, weight and reach advantage. I swear my mum was pregnant for about three years. Even though there was a two-year age gap we were always the same height, until our young adulthood when I stayed at 5-foot-8 and Joe zoomed to 6-foot-3.

The boxing felt totally normal growing up but my wife was horrified when she found out and saw the photo. My daughters will be four and six this Christmas and they are a similar size, so it would be a fair fight, but I can't think of anything worse that watching them punch each other in the face. I would rather eat 27 Ferrero Rocher and watch *Strictly* than see my children box. Maybe I'm becoming a big middle-class softie.

The main problem when we fought at Christmas was the lack of a mouthguard, as my teeth genuinely couldn't fit in a child-size mouthguard. I have had my two front teeth since the age of five, and if you think my teeth look big now, they looked enormous in the gob of a five-year-old. I was called 'Tombstone Teeth' at school and I couldn't argue with that name. That's exactly what they looked like. I've never really been that bothered by jokes about my teeth. They are fairly white and straight but big. The only thing that annoys me is the quality or accuracy of a joke. The old pub joke 'he could eat an apple through a letterbox' simply doesn't work in relation to my teeth. That joke only works if you have protruding buck teeth. Yes, I have big teeth: call me a horse, call me Tombstone Teeth, call me Rylan. But from an analytical comedy point of view, the apple letterbox joke doesn't work.

My teeth have become part of my brand as a comedian. If you google 'big teeth comedian' or 'big teeth blond', I will be the first result. And not just the first – I dominate the results. As a word of caution, however, I would like to make you aware that if you do google 'big teeth blond', you will also pull up a number of links to hardcore pornographic websites featuring big teeth blond(e)s, both male and female, getting up to all sorts of filth. I mean it's very eye-opening, to say the least. I obviously only briefly checked out seven or eight websites on a strictly business-research basis. Merry Christmas, everyone.

So far on this earth I have enjoyed and in some cases endured 35 different Christmases. Some with stolen goods, some in semi-silence with awkward middle-class chats with in-laws, and others with Yorkshire puddings launched at my face. As a family, me, Lou and the kids have settled on a nice working-class and middle-class Christmas combination that we are all happy with. A compromise, if you will. Sure, most of the ideas are Lou's and I am not bullied but encouraged into agreeing with those ideas – but a compromise, nonetheless.

One thing I have noticed about Christmas is that whatever your background and whoever you are, the reason we love that time of year is the same. It's a celebration of survival – another year done together as a family. Life is hard whatever your circumstances, and getting through the year deserves to be toasted. So we all sit round the table with our families eating and drinking merrily, with silly hats on, pulling crackers. Whether the crackers are from Poundland or Harrods, it doesn't really make a difference. It's the person who's still there at the dinner table pulling it with you that makes the difference.

FAMILY NETWORKS

Things I did before I started writing this chapter

....

PACK OF MALTESERS

....

2 BISCUITS

....

COFFEE

....

GLASS OF MILK

....

**DELETED SOME PHOTOS FROM MY
DAUGHTER'S IPAD TO FREE UP STORAGE**

....

DISHWASHER

....

GOOGLED 'HOW OLD IS KIERAN TIERNEY?'

....

TWITTER SEARCHED 'LOCKDOWN 3'

....

I think family networks are one of the biggest differences in the class system. As the old saying goes, it's not what you know, it's who you know. My children will have such a different pool of people available to talk to them and give advice compared to what I had growing up. I wouldn't call it better or worse, just different. It's great to have a godfather who works in nuclear science if you want to work in nuclear science, but if you want to be a carpenter he can't really help.

Growing up, we were surrounded by mechanics, cab drivers, fishmongers, gas fitters and lorry drivers. One of the most impressive people we knew, someone my dad used to boast about knowing, was Gary the Lift. Now, Gal was so impressive because he was a lorry driver friend of my dad's who could – drum roll, please – change the wheel on an artic lorry on his own, hence the nickname 'the Lift'. Artic is short for articulated lorry, for the confused upper classes reading this. It's basically the biggest road lorry they do in the UK. First and foremost, this lorry wheel-changing is hugely impressive just as a feat of strength, almost like a qualifying round of *World's Strongest Man*, as he would actually lift and pull the wheel off the lorry itself rather than use the metal bars to wiggle it off. While on paper it might be more beneficial as a family to have a friend high up in government or a lawyer, if you're my dad trapped on the hard shoulder of the A2 in a lorry with a tyre that needs changing, it is an absolute godsend to have old long-arm Gary in your phone book.

I should also say that my dad and his pals used to drive these 44-ton lorries with no power steering – something that I think needs to be said, acknowledged and respected. I struggle with a parallel park with cameras and sensors. I am a terrible driver and to this day I think my dad is slightly disappointed in me for never learning to drive a manual car. I did my test in an automatic. Oh, the shame. I don't really understand having a car with gears. I get it if you have a classic sports car and you want to change gears going through country lanes. But I was knocking about in a 12-year-old Nissan Micra in South East London. There's not much thrill in crunching through the gears of a 1.2 litre Japanese nanna car at an average speed of 9 mph.

In my opinion all cars should be electric and automatic. Changing gears is such a waste of time. I have too much on my to-do list without adding a gear change to it. Why are we still changing gear when everything in life is done for you now? Even Google knows what you want and predicts your searches. If you order a pizza, a pizza arrives, not a bag of flour and tomatoes. I also refuse to check oil. When the car starts smoking or doesn't start, I might pop my head under the bonnet, but not before I've called my dad so he can tell me what I'm actually looking for.

As well as lorry-tyre-lifting legends, my dad also had a load of hard mates. He grew up in South East London in the 1950s and went to school with the Richardsons, a notorious tough family. But it seems like everyone went to school with the Richardsons in South London, the same way that every baby boomer in East London knew the Kray twins. I wouldn't call my dad a hard man but let's put it this way, he wouldn't be shy to defend himself if necessary. Growing up, there was a great sense of primal security in knowing that my dad and his friends could look after us if needed. A security I absolutely cannot offer my daughters. I'm as soft as anything and will always try to defuse a situation before I inevitably run away as fast as I can.

It's a strange experience becoming famous and still living in a rough area. The first big TV show I did was the spin off to *I'm a Celebrity … Get Me Out of Here!* which was given the catchy title *I'm a Celebrity … Get Me Out of Here! Now!* It is the longest name for a TV show in the world and a pain in the arse to type, but great to help me hit the 70 to 80,000 word count I'm contractually obliged to reach. I mean, let's face it, that means 70,000. Surely no one has ever hit the 80,000, have they? Or even more incredibly, someone banging out 85,000 and needing to reduce? Anyway, I did *I'm a Celebrity … Get Me Out of Here! Now!* which was on ITV2 and got 1.5 million viewers every night for three weeks, as it was on straight after the main show, *I'm a Celebrity … Get Me Out of Here!* I loved working on *I'm a Celebrity … Get Me Out of Here! Now!* (Am I taking the piss here? Okay, I'll stop.)

I came back from Australia and I was instantly someone off the telly. I lived in New Cross at the time and people would shout at me from vans, 'It's the geezer with all the teeth from the jungle!' Which made me sound like some shaman who stole teeth from people in a jungle. I wasn't famous enough for people to know my name. They just sort of knew my face from somewhere, and people would stare at me for uncomfortably long periods of time. As I was living a stone's throw from the home of Millwall Football Club, I expected them to say, 'Oi, what you fucking looking at?' then try to fight me. Even now, if someone stares at me I just assume they will want to fight me at any moment.

Growing up, the question, 'Oi, what you looking at?' would be the stuff of nightmares. It's impossible to answer. If you say, 'No one,' they would say, 'So I'm a nobody, am I?' and then that would start a fight. So then if you say, 'Actually, I've changed my mind, I was looking at you,' they would say, 'What you looking at me for, you mug?' Then a fight would start. So I would try to avoid all of this palaver by never making eye contact with anyone. If I did make eye contact and it got awkward I would try to be funny to ease the tension. If that didn't work, I would run away like a pussy. Whereas my dad would stand his ground.

My dad once told us a story about when he was in the pub with his pal Freddie, who was a small but hard bloke. Now, considering that my dad is 5-foot-7 and he's calling his mate small, in my head I'm picturing a combo of Warwick Davis and Danny DeVito sitting in the corner of the Dog and Arsehole sipping a John Smith's.

Poor Freddie was complaining to my dad about how someone had been jumping his fence and stealing his clothes off the washing line. This had been happening for a couple of weeks to the whole street. They had a few more beers and then a group of eight lads walked into the pub. As the lads got a round in Freddie noticed something. 'He's wearing my fucking shirt, Dave,' he said. My dad panicked as Freddie marched towards the eight fellas. It turned out that these eight blokes were travellers, so after exchanging words they offered Freddie the chance to fight the man for the shirt, which he agreed to. So now my dad was the cornerman for Freddie in an old-school straightener outside the pub. In Freddie's opponents' corner were seven men, so he had it all covered: trainer, cut man, spit-bucket carrier plus extras. My dad was panicking because if it turned nasty it was 8 vs 2, and as tough as my dad and Freddie were, combined they were only 9-foot-3. However, it played out a fair fight, like the travellers promised. Freddie even got the better of the tussle. He got his shirt back, they shook hands and all went back in the pub to have a drink together.

Now, some people would say, 'Ah, the good old days – a nice honest straightener.' But I'm very different to my dad. I don't find it a funny story from back in the day. I find it absolutely petrifying. If I managed to find myself in that situation now, with someone walking into a pub with seven friends wearing a shirt they had stolen off me, I would get up, apologise to the men and leave that pub immediately with a bright red face. But this story of my dad's is told at family gatherings as a funny story. Does my dad really find it funny or is he using humour to deal with a traumatic experience? Why is my reaction to this situation so different to my dad's? We are similar in character, we have the same genes. What's the difference maker? Is it class? Is it upbringing?

There is no doubt about it, my dad had a much tougher childhood and adolescence than me. The poor sod couldn't read or write and was driving a van at 13. He had to fight and struggle all his life to give me and my brothers the opportunities and lifestyle we have benefited from. Both of my parents have worked so hard and given us boys everything and anything they could to help us. The sacrifices they made enabled all of their children to go on to have successful careers and loving families. We owe them a lot. There hasn't always been the money there, but physically and emotionally the bank was never empty.

Now that I have a comfortable life I can avoid a fight over a shirt, and it's easy to be financially stable and judge people for it. But if you're skint and someone literally takes the shirt from your back, it's about more than the shirt at that point. It's a pride and survival thing. If you let someone take your shirt one week, next week they will come back for your trousers.

Here's another one that, looking back, is a rather bleak story but again is another one of my dad's funny anecdotes. It would normally start with an uncle or cousin requesting the story from my dad: 'Dave, tell them the other one about you and the fridge.' We didn't have a fridge. Ours had broken. But it was winter so we were keeping stuff in the garden until we could afford a new one. As luck would have it, one of my dad's friends had an old one that we could have for free. I can't remember who it was, but knowing my dad he probably had a mad name like Mick the Tick. Anyway, the 'funny family anecdote' goes like this: my dad went to pick up the fridge in his van but on the way home he got into a road-rage altercation with two blokes. He had a fight with them and the two blokes won, and while my dad was on the floor they nicked the fridge.

Now, even though I'm claiming that this story is not funny, as I typed it out it did make me laugh a bit. So, I have to admit that I find it funny, even though I don't know why. Maybe it's the imagery of my dad on the floor as two men carry a fridge and try to squeeze it into the back of a Mini Cooper. I've made it a Mini Cooper in my head so that it's funnier when I close my eyes. I have tried to tell this story in my stand-up shows and people just gasp and worry rather than laugh. Especially in Cambridge. They are the poshest crowd in the country. Lovely caring people who, even when they laugh, do it politely. Sometimes they just smile and make no noise. That's enough sometimes for a Cambridge audience – a big open-mouthed, silent-grin laugh.

I was oblivious to the power of a connected family growing up. I only really acknowledged that it was a thing when I went to the Edinburgh Fringe festival, which is a strange combo of all kinds of Scottish people up there watching shows mixed in with the poshest and most middle-class English people you could find. I didn't even know that the Edinburgh Fringe existed until I was 24. I started doing open-mic comedy and everyone said that if you want to make it you've got to go to Edinburgh. I was so confused. I was in London already, where the majority of the agents, telly people and gigs were. Why would I need to go to Edinburgh to find them when the comedy industry was based right here in London? Then someone explained to me what the Edinburgh Fringe was. Even now I don't really understand it.

Basically, the whole population of Edinburgh leave town for August and rent out their homes to middle- and upper-class 18–25-year-olds from England at a huge profit. People moan about this but I think good on the locals. If it was the other way round and Bromley was home to the biggest arts festival in the world and loads of poshos turned up in Barbour jackets and red trousers, I'd overcharge them too. Plus make them pay extra to park their Land Rover Defender on my drive.

The fringe is host to a number of university comedy troupes. I think troupe is French for 'unfunny improv shit'. Along with the uni shows there are thousands of shows available to watch, including music, magic, plays and, of course, stand-up comedy shows. Up-and-coming comedians take a 60-minute show up to Scotland and perform it every night for three weeks. A vast number of agents, bookers and TV commissioners attend the Fringe to find the next star of stage and screen. It's like a huge trade fair essentially, but it's hugely costly, which makes it incredibly hard for someone from a lower-income background to participate in.

I've got a little bit of a chip on my shoulder when it comes to Edinburgh. I found it a frustrating place to perform. It felt like a big network of people who were all connected to each other somehow, which if you were a part of made everything a lot easier – all the boring stuff like travel, accommodation and socialising. Someone would have a spare room going or someone's godfather was coming up to take them out for dinner. Or they would have been brought up to the Fringe as a child with their parents.

As someone from a working-class background it's almost impossible to infiltrate and understand what is going on at the Fringe. It's the equivalent of a posh kid from Oxford who goes to boarding school trying to become a member of a football hooligan firm. Even if he is proper hard and desperate for a tear-up, he won't have the first idea how to get involved. He won't know anyone to take him to the game. He won't know which pub all the faces meet at. He won't know what to wear or how to speak in order to fit in. He will be utterly clueless, turning up to the wrong stadium dressed as a full-kit wanker with a half-and-half scarf and a Stone Island beanie hat, shouting, 'You want some? I'll give it to ya!' That's who I was in Edinburgh, a desperate full-kit wanker wanting to be a comedian but with no guidance or advice on how to go about it.

If my kids now wanted to perform at the Fringe, I could tell them where to stay, where to get posters and flyers, when to book the train tickets to get the cheapest fare. But that's because they are not working class. They are middle-class children with a dad who is somehow heavily involved in the arts with links and contacts to hundreds of people in the industry. Give me an hour on the phone and I could have a venue, accommodation, PR and a promoter sorted.

While it might only take me an hour now, it's taken me 12 years in the business to get those contacts. Did knowing nothing and having no one to help me in the industry mean that I had to really want it and work harder? Or was I always going to want it and work hard, and if I'd had a big contact book when I started would I have become successful quicker or easier? We will never know for sure, but I do think my naivety and ignorance did also benefit me. Plus, being working class and different definitely helped me stand out in that world – like the posh boarding-school hooligan. He might not be the best hooligan in the firm, but you're not going to forget the posh boy in full kit squaring up to the Chelsea Headhunters at Euston station.

As much as I found performing at the Fringe challenging, as a punter it is incredible. It's one of the greatest places on earth if you love comedy. It's so exciting – you can feel the energy of young, ambitious people all taking a chance on themselves. I loved it so much. You could watch comedy from 10 a.m. until 4 a.m. all day, every day for a month. I was in heaven. Again, as a visitor it's still pricey, as hotels costs a lot. I'm talking Center Parcs in August levels. On top of the accommodation costs, most of the shows are £10–15 a ticket. The introduction of the Free Fringe in the last 15 years has been brilliant. It's a much cheaper way for new acts to put on a show with free entry, asking instead for a donation in the bucket as the audience leave the venue, like a busker or street performer would.

I did the Free Fringe and had the time of my life walking up and down the Royal Mile for hours, giving out flyers to random strangers. I could get a room full every day just from talking them into it. At that point I had no show or jokes, but I always had a full room. I was a market-stall trader doing a comedy show. But that's how you learn to be a stand-up. What I found frustrating was making the move into a venue where people would have to buy a £10 ticket to come to your show. This brought a very different crowd. On the Free Fringe you got students, tourists and people on a budget. Being in a paid venue meant that you got more of a 'Fringe audience'.

The Edinburgh Fringe is a strange bubble where it's not really enough just to be funny. The shows that do well need to have a meaning or a journey, and if it's funny it's a bonus. The Fringe audience want to think and feel challenged and clever at the end of a show. The truth is that sometimes the word 'boner' is enough to make you laugh, without any greater meaning. For me, as a performer and an audience member, all I want is funny. If the show has a greater meaning that's great but not essential for me. You get a lot of middle-class twenty-somethings in a Fringe audience who do a lot of sitting in coffee shops on Twitter, having opinions. The Fringe audience love an opinion and a debate.

Alongside the younger guys are the old-school Fringe-goers. I'm talking *Telegraph*-reading golf-club members dressed in Cath Kidston and Cotton Traders rugby tops. You would get these guys during the week and then at the weekends the Scottish locals would come out, which was brilliant because you got a much broader, more mainstream audience. Plus some working-class people, which made me feel homesick. Lots of the more alternative acts would hate weekends because of the mainstream crowds. But I loved it, as it felt like people were coming out to have a fun night of entertainment, whereas in the week the Fringe audience wanted a good old think about life.

I remember doing a late show at Edinburgh on a Saturday, and me and a couple of acts that will remain nameless were walking to the venue where we could see the audience queuing up. They were very rowdy and drunk, and the other two acts were panicking. They kept saying, 'Oh my God, look at the state of the audience. They are all drunk chavs, look at them! This is going to be awful. You'll be all right, Rob, but we are going to struggle.'

Basically they saw working-class people and shat themselves. They assumed that just because I was working class I would have a good gig. In their defence I had my best gig of the whole festival. I was so excited to be in front of what I perceived as 'normal people'.

Believe it or not I struggled to connect with the traditional Fringe audience. I mean, who could have predicted that? A little commoner doing observations on working-class life to loads of middle-class people. I didn't read the *Guardian*, I didn't like rugby, I didn't even know what Radio 4 was. I didn't stand a chance. I was so confused and down about it. I couldn't understand how I was able to travel all around the country and perform in different comedy clubs successfully but not in Edinburgh, where it just wasn't working as well and I really struggled to feel a connection with the audience.

I wasn't deluded. I had done a bit of telly at this point. I had won a number of new comedian competitions and I was establishing myself on the circuit. I had been signed by an agent. So I knew I had good stuff but it just wasn't working. Then I had a moment of realisation halfway through the festival. During the Fringe you share a venue with about eight other acts and you all have a time slot. I was on at 6 p.m. in this small 50-seater venue and I was selling about 15 tickets a day. Before me was a sketch group I had never heard of before this festival – and it's a pretty small world. I couldn't believe that they were sold out and received a standing ovation every day. I could hear their set as I waited for my turn to go on. It was a good show but not sold-out-and-standing-ovation good. It made me question everything, because I don't know much, but I do know funny. It's all I know. I love it and have dedicated my life to it for the last 20 years.

I also understand that it's subjective and there is comedy I don't particularly enjoy but I can see why a certain demographic love it. But listening to the show I was just thinking, *That's not good enough to warrant that response*. Now, when I say standing ovation, this wasn't a normal standing ovation. The noise was like they'd resurrected Elvis and Tupac Shakur for the encore. It was bedlam in there. I couldn't work it out, so I stood by the door as the audience left to see who these loud people were and if I could get them to come to my show with my trusty flyers. But as they left, it didn't feel like an audience leaving a show. It felt like the end of a wedding. The audience were kissing and cuddling the performers, saying things like, 'Wonderful stuff, I'm going to text your mother now to say how brilliant you are.' 'Great work, darling. Tabitha is coming up next week with her five friends from home. I've bought them all tickets for the show. Bravo.'

I was just thinking, *What the fuck is going on?* It was like I had infiltrated a cult. *Who are these people and what are they talking about? What is a Tabitha? Is it a name or the apron dinner ladies wear?* I still hadn't met a Rupert at this stage of my life. Then I realised that Edinburgh in August is like the Costa del Sol for posh people. They all go there separately but they all know each other and meet up. They all go and see their friends' kids' shows to demonstrate their support, while – I imagine – hoping it's shit so they can slag it off in a separate WhatsApp group afterwards.

As much as I was jealous of this support network other performers had, I did feel sorry for the parents. Imagine going to Edinburgh and your best friend's kid is in an awful play and you are forced out of politeness to go and watch it. It must be absolutely horrendous. Or, even worse, knowing your kid is unfunny and being forced to sit through an hour-long show. What do you say to your kid in that situation? Silently continue to support them or pull them to one side and break the news to them. 'Sorry about this, kiddo. I'm your dad and I will always love you, but fuck me you're shit. Let's knock it on the head and try something else, pottery or gymnastics or something.'

I've always said that my daughters can be anything they want to be as long as they are happy. I don't care what sexuality they are, what gender they are – I would even forgive them for being Tottenham Hotspur fans. But the only thing that would force me to disown them is if they formed an improv sketch group at the Edinburgh Fringe. I couldn't do it. I'd have to be honest with them. 'I'm out, kids. Find a new dad. I'm divorcing your mum and I'm going to start a new family, and it's all your fault, girls. Remember that.'

I would love to say, 'Of course, I'm joking.' But I'm really not. Singing, dancing, juggling, acting, stand-up, I'm there for you, girls. But sketch improv I can't handle. It goes against everything I stand for.

This support network for middle- and upper-class kids used to make me really angry. Now I am much calmer about it and understand that it's not their fault, it's just the lifestyle they were born into. The same way I was born into a different set of circumstances. You can't be mad at someone for something they can't control. I think I was frustrated because I was so aggressively desperate for success, as it was my way out of being skint. I had invested every penny I had in Edinburgh and gigged every moment of every day to get the most out of the festival. I was still working full-time in a dead-end office job and I used up all my holiday to go to the festival. I would be doing these mixed-bill comedy shows, watching 20-year-olds turn up late for gigs, hungover, not do the full time expected of them, not bother flyering and then, if they were tired, cancel a show without a care in the world. I was so angry, as I just saw it as wasting potential stage time for me and other people who were serious about comedy.

The only way to become a comedian is by getting as much stage time as possible, and I was desperate for it. Stage time for me came before anything; it was the only way to get better. One Christmas, I drove to Northampton to do five minutes for free, not even petrol money – just for the stage time. I was an animal for any opportunity I could get. At the Fringe I would have to watch these people not making the most of the opportunity they had on stage. I used to think, *Either take it seriously and be committed or get the fuck out of my way. This is my way out! I've not got time to play about.* But then it dawned on me that the reason they behaved like that was because they actually didn't have a care in the world. Their parents would pay for their accommodation and production costs, on top of their monthly allowance. Not in all cases, but in a lot of cases. It was like a posh kids' summer camp, in essence. 'Off you go to the Fringe, Jasper, and have some fun before you study law at Durham.' Which in reality is absolutely fine, what a great position to be in to be able to offer your kid that experience. But back then I was skint, ambitious, angry and obsessed with progress, and I couldn't see or feel anything other than frustration.

I don't think the working-class chip on my shoulder will ever go. It just swells or shrinks, depending on the atmosphere. Very much like how a penis changes size in hot and cold weather. The Edinburgh Fringe was like the Sahara Desert for my knob. A huge working-class chip on my boner. See, boner is a really funny word, isn't it?

The strange thing about class is that, while it does exist in the rest of the world, it's much clearer cut and obvious in the UK. In countries like the USA and Australia it's much more defined by rich and poor people. Whereas in the UK money plays a part but connections, family history and education also define class.

The Adelaide Fringe festival in Australia is totally different to the Edinburgh Fringe festival, even though it's essentially the same event. In some cases, there will be the exact same shows being performed at Edinburgh and Adelaide. But there is a much more relaxed feel to performing in Australia. The audiences are there to have fun. There is no academic or analytical weight added to the Fringe. It's just a month in the year when all sorts of madness descends on Adelaide: magic, drag and comedy. You buy a ticket, enjoy the show and then have a beer in the beautiful sunshine. Don't get me wrong, Edinburgh is an incredible city, but it's got a long way to go to beat an Australian summer.

I went to Adelaide in 2011 after winning a competition at the Edinburgh Fringe. The prize for the winner was a return flight to Adelaide, free accommodation and someone to produce my show for free. This was an incredible moment for me, as I was absolutely brassic. I had literally spent all my money on going to Edinburgh and I had quit my job in an office to pursue comedy. I was living in a house share in Lewisham and comedy was just about paying my £300 a month rent. I was living the dream: I was a professional comedian. All the money I earned came from comedy and it was just enough to keep me afloat.

However, there were a few problems. When I say I was skint, I was proper skint. Not middle-class or upper-class skint, when you have spent your month's salary but deep down you know you can access your savings, sell some stuff on eBay or borrow off your parents. I am talking proper skint. Zero pounds in the bank skint. Sold anything that could be worth something at a boot sale skint. This is no dig at my parents. They would give me their last pound and I think they have in the past. But I was too proud to ask and, also, I knew deep down that there wasn't any going spare to borrow. The strange thing about your dad being self-employed is that if you do ask for money you feel instant guilt, as you know it means he literally has to leave the house, get in the taxi and earn it. Being skint was okay in the UK, as I could always do some office temp work or pick up extra gigs. However, in Adelaide I knew no one.

The flight there was fine and I got picked up from the airport by the production team, then they dropped me off at the accommodation. Now, free accommodation always sounds good but the issue is that it's always shit, isn't it? For four weeks I lived in a hostel with shared bathrooms and 15 international students who only spoke Punjabi. The venue where I was performing was at the town hall, a 20-minute tram journey away, so for the first week of the festival I bunked the fare on my way to the venue. I couldn't afford it – I didn't just love the buzz of a free ride. That's quite a stressful start to your run of 21 shows.

On top of that I arrived at the venue to find out I was performing an hour-long solo show. Back in the UK I had been told it was a 20-minute set in a mixed bill with other comedians. I had done my first ever gig 18 months previously and I only had 15 minutes of jokes – I thought I could blag an extra 5 minutes chatting to the crowd. But now I was doing my first solo show and had to invent 45 minutes of material. This was a fucking disaster. It seems funny now on paper, but I was a volcanic ball of anxiety at the time. I found this out about 45 minutes before I did my first show on opening night, so I had 45 minutes to write 45 minutes of jokes. In comedy there are so many times and numbers – that's mainly what comedy is. How many are in the audience? What time am I on? How long am I doing? I wanted to cry and run away. I would have got a cab to the airport if I could have afforded it.

I did manage to 'fill' the hour that night and I'm going to tell you how. Firstly, though, I would like to apologise to the seven people in the crowd. Can seven people be a crowd? I don't know, but those seven felt like a baying mob of hooligans. This is what I did. First and foremost, I started 6 minutes late and finished 6 minutes early. That's

12 minutes covered with zero talking. Phew! I played a 5-minute walk-on track, which I introduced myself over for ages. The joke being look how long he's taking to introduce himself, isn't that funny? In truth it was a scared boy talking for survival.

I did my solid 15 minutes of material, but really, really, really, REALLY slowly, which took 25 minutes. I can't express how slowly I did my material. I would guess some audiences might at some point have wondered whether I had a speech problem or if I was seconds away from having a stroke. We are up to 42 minutes of the show filled now. With the final 18 minutes I spoke to the audience. At a much greater speed than I had done earlier, which must have confused the audience as well as bringing relief to those who thought they had paid 15 dollars to witness a medical emergency. Now, I didn't do 'crowd work' like Ross Noble does crowd work. For those not familiar with Mr Noble, his style of comedy is to get one piece of information from the audience and then go on a full 20-minute improvised routine that finishes in a huge laugh and a massive round of applause. My crowd work at the time consisted of literally just speaking to them like we were in a queue at the supermarket. I am getting itchy and stressed just thinking about this gig.

I know you want a bit of good news in this Adelaide story. It's coming, but not yet. The next day I went to the beach to try to cheer up and think about some new material. That last part went well, as I wrote loads of new jokes in the sun. I got home feeling good, only to realise that the Aussie sun has got a bit more of a kick to it than the sun in Margate. Even though it's the same sun. Mad, innit? My back was medically burnt, third-degree burns type of burnt, and the saddest part was that I didn't know anyone I could ask to put the aftersun cream on my back. It's a fairly intimate thing, the cream-to-back relationship. Strictly only acceptable for mums and partners to apply. The first lads' holiday to Kos when you all realise you have to do each other's sun cream is an awkward moment. Such an awkward laddie yet needy exchange.

'Oi Oi, let's go to bar street and do some shots.'

'Mate, can you put some cream on my back?'

'Yeah, course. You do me and I'll do you. Just don't let the other lads see.'

So how did I put the aftersun cream on my bright red blistered back in order to soothe the pain? Well, I'm glad you asked. I went to the privacy of my bedroom, which had two single beds and tiled floors. Yep, that's right, my bedroom had tiled floors and a spare single bed in it. It also had one stained-glass window, as the accommodation was a church that had been renovated to house 24 Asian business studies students as well as a depressed, burnt, scared boy from South East London. So, I squeezed the aftersun directly on the floor and lay down and rubbed my back on it like a bear scratching its back on a big oak tree. That's how it felt in my head but I think the reality was quite different. I was less powerful bear and more a pathetic slimy eel that had recently been caught and was wriggling for his life on the cream-covered tiled floor of a hostel.

Don't worry, good news is coming. Still not yet, though. About two days later I felt a bit rough and couldn't eat my Crunchy Nut Corn Flakes and milk, which was what I ate for breakfast, lunch and dinner every day. This was due to my tight budget coupled with the fact that I'm a fat, greedy boy deep down. Part of me almost loved the fact that I could only afford sugary cereal. Also, it was helpful to consume that much sugar to keep my teeth from becoming too healthy. Imagine how big my teeth would be without all that sugar and decay. Anyway, I googled a doctor's, which was a 20-minute tram ride or an hour's walk away in 30 degrees. I jumped on the tram, saw a ticket inspector and jumped off immediately. *60 minutes walk it is*, I thought. The doctor confirmed that I had a throat and chest infection and he gave me antibiotics, a $150 bill and then slapped my arse and off I went on another hour-long walk home. This was the lowest part of the trip. I wanted to swallow my pride and call my parents for help, but my throat was too inflamed for that. So I gulped the best I could and got on with it. During that time my then girlfriend and future wife Lou sent me parcels and letters and so did my parents, which helped so much. My accommodation felt a little bit like prison so all correspondence was greatly received. My mum sent me a toothbrush, which I managed to melt down into a shank for protection.

Once the antibiotics had taken effect the happy part of this story kicked into gear. Now, reading this chapter might make you feel like you need a connected family or a network to succeed in life or an industry. Which is in part true, but if you're lucky and look in the right places and are open with others you realise that there are some really good people in this world. They aren't networkers and they aren't trying to take advantage; some people are just good people because they are good people.

The show had been getting better and better, as during the day I had two options: sit and write better jokes or lie in bed and cry. So, after a couple of hours of crying I would knock out some more jokes and the show gradually got funnier. Onstage my confidence was growing by the day. By the middle of the run I had an hour-long show that I was really proud of. I had some money coming in, as I had picked up some paid gig work at the Fringe. Enough to afford the tram and the occasional vegetable to go with my cereal. But I was slowly slipping into depression. Onstage I was flying but offstage I was still feeling very vulnerable and overwhelmed by it all. I didn't know anyone in Adelaide and I didn't have any money to go anywhere or do anything. If I'd had some extra income I could have gone shopping or out on day trips, but I only had enough for essentials. I was chronically lonely and sad all day until my show.

During one show I noticed a guy in the front row in his forties with a shaved head and tattoos – exactly my kind of audience member. He was laughing along with this teenage girl. After the show he came up to me to tell me how much he'd enjoyed the show. He seemed like a nice bloke, though I had slight concerns that he was a pervy wrong'un until he introduced me to his teenage daughter – not his girlfriend. THANK GOD.

The bloke was a man called Ross Howat, originally from Coventry, now living in Adelaide with his wife and three daughters. He bought me a drink and we chatted about the show and my time in Adelaide. I think he could tell I wasn't happy. I have always been an easy person to read, as I have no filter between my feelings and my face. I am terrible at poker. I get so excited when I get a good hand that the excitement starts bubbling out of me. I can't help it. I think being easy to read has helped me to be a good comedian, as I love stand-up so much and it's genuine joy in my eyes and face when I perform. However, that isn't how I feel 24/7, especially when I was in Adelaide after the show. I always think you can tell when someone isn't happy by looking into their eyes. You can smile and laugh but if you're unhappy your eyes are the first to tell on you.

From that moment Ross Howat, originally from Coventry, wasn't just living in Adelaide with his wife and three daughters. Ross Howat, originally from Coventry, was living in Adelaide with his wife and three daughters and 25-year-old adopted son. There was no official paperwork or public statement but I had been adopted. I knew it and the Howats knew it. Over the next two weeks he would pick me up from my cell for all sorts of day trips. I went to his house for dinner, we went to the beach and on a boat trip. Sometimes I remember just sitting in their house watching telly and it was bliss. I used to look forward to him picking me up so much. He came to watch the show a number of times with family and friends, always insisting on paying and never taking a free ticket.

I am actually getting emotional thinking about it. I don't think I ever really comprehended the impact it had on me. Adelaide had been such a traumatic experience until I met him that I think I buried it under the carpet and tried to forget about it. Going to a foreign country on the other side of the world to do a show I hadn't written, with no support network or financial way to get home if I needed to was a crazy move. Of course I struggled. That was always going to be a difficult time for someone. As a father now, I realise what that family did for me is priceless, and without them I might have done something silly and irreversible in that hostel. Back in 2011, I was just a lost scared boy in Adelaide. There was no ulterior motive from Ross and his family other than looking after someone who needed help. I had no money, no fame and nothing to offer them. It was a one-way street of altruism and I will always be thankful.

I will return to the Adelaide Fringe one day and I can't wait to take the Howats out for dinner and on a boat trip to try to pay them back. But the truth is that no money, gesture or networked connection will ever be able to match what they did for me. We're still in touch on WhatsApp, keeping each other updated on our families. My daughters are obsessed with the Australian cartoon show *Bluey*, but you can't get any of the merchandise in the UK, so they sent over a big box of *Bluey* pyjamas, books and teddies. In return I have sent things they miss from the UK, which include Monster Munch, Mini Cheddars and Iced Gems, along with 3 to 5 kilos of cocaine hidden among it all. Apparently Aussie coke is crap. It's the least I can do for them.

I should add that Julia Chamberlain, a comedy promoter and critic, was also very kind to me during that time. Sensing that I was alone and sad, she took me for lunch and always invited me out for drinks. Along with her and the Howats, comedians Steve Hall, Jimmy McGhie and Daniel Kitson looked after me, bought me dinner and let me hang around with them, and I will always be grateful. The weird thing was that even though I was in the middle of a period of depression, my show was nominated for the best newcomer award, which is a pretty big deal in the industry but I had no management or PR team to tell me. I only found out on the day of the awards show, when my sound technician asked me if I was going to it. Awards aren't really my thing – I'm more about the process of making comedy, not the accolades – but as soon as I found out I was nominated I decided I loved awards and found the venue for where the awards were being held. I tried to get in but my name wasn't on the guest list, even though I was nominated, which I thought was mental. So I asked the lady on the door if they had announced the winner of the best newcomer. She said, 'Yes, they have,' and I asked who it was. All I can remember her saying is a name that wasn't 'Rob Beckett', so I left and bunked the tram fare back to my Asian business-studies church-hostel to give my burnt back the creamy tiled floor treatment one last time before I flew home.

I sometimes think how different my experience in Adelaide would have been if my parents were richer or middle or upper class, with connections in comedy. If I had known people in Adelaide it could have helped me. I could have stayed in better accommodation where I would have felt safe and comfortable. I would have been able to pay for my tram fare and for taxis to and from the doctor's. I might not have been loving every second of my time there, but it takes the pressure off when you're not anxious about avoiding ticket inspectors on your commute. What impact would it have had on my career?

I think if I'd had access to money before I met the Howats I would have booked the first flight to London and returned home immediately. I remember spending hours on hold trying to bring my flight home forward by one day once the Fringe had ended, but I couldn't do it because there was a fee to change it. I was so done with it I couldn't face one extra day in the Australian sun – the desperate actions of a desperate man. But then I think the other side of the argument is that the experience was character building. Maybe the hardship and struggle made me stronger and more resilient. I might have been happier if I'd gone home, but I would have missed out on the opportunity to perform an hour-long set for 21 days in a row. Stage time like that early in your career is crucial to progressing and learning your craft. Twenty-one hours of stage time would have taken me two or three years to get in London on the open-mic circuit. I managed to acquire that stage time in three weeks.

Is it character building to be scared and worried all the time? Is it character building to be bailed out by mum and dad and run away back to the family home to hide, knowing that you quit when things got tough? Where would I be now if I'd given up and gone home? We will never know, but luckily for me I met the Howats, so I didn't give up. But one thing I do know for sure is: always wear sunscreen, kids! That big, yellow bastard in the sky doesn't take any prisoners.

EDUCATION

Things I did before I started writing this chapter

••••••••••••••••••••••••••••

BUILD AN ENTIRE LAMBORGHINI OUT OF
LEGO THAT TOOK NINE DAYS

••••••••••••••••••••••••••••

I didn't learn much at the secondary school I went to. It was a typical comprehensive, lots of fighting and plenty of drama. The one thing I did learn was an almost sixth sense for being able to predict a fight. I can be in a pub and, 30 seconds before it kicks off, I will have foreseen it and made my exit. Growing up in South East London, I think you learn how to fight or how to escape. I chose escape.

The mad thing that I remember about school was that the only way you could gain status was through being tough, good at football and/or good-looking. If you were clever you were bullied for being a nerd or ignored. I couldn't imagine a world where being intelligent at school was an asset that could give you status and make you popular. It was only when I started doing comedy shows with really intelligent, confident comedians from private schools and grammar schools that I realised intelligence at some schools is admired. I would think, *How is this nerd so confident? They are so proud of being smart. They would have got annihilated at my school with this swagger.* A protective part of me wanted to say to them,

'All right, mate, calm it down a bit. I get it, you're clever and know loads of stuff, but people can hear you. You're gonna make yourself a target.'

There's a really clear divide in the comedy industry between the stiff-neck and loose-neck comedians. It's normally defined by ability in academia more than intelligence. All comedians are intelligent. We might not have common sense or social skills but you have to have a certain level of intelligence to be a comedian. It's too hard to fluke it every time. There's a lot going on to control and if you don't have a brain it's never going to work.

Before I discuss the differences between loose and stiff necks, I want to make it clear that both stiff-neck and loose-neck comedians are funny. There is no favouritism here, it's just a different approach to creating comedy. The stiff-neck comedians love to prepare and write out their routines in full. Some might not love it but it's the most effective way for them to work. Sometimes on an actual computer in Word documents. I know, an actual computer! It's enough to make a loose-neck comic instantly vomit. The stiffies then hone their gear over time in public to create a bulletproof script they know works and is multi-layered and structured, all tied together in one seamless narrative. Though if you put a stiff neck on the spot with a heckle or a distraction they can panic because it hasn't been planned or prepared for.

The loose-neck comedians, however, could write for hours before a show but once they are onstage it would become clear that everything they have written is crap. They are much funnier performing and creating in the moment, and their best comedy is born onstage and develops each time they perform. It's a much more loose and organic way to write jokes. After months of gigs they will have a comedy show that is very funny and effective but only exists in their head and on scraps of paper. Both approaches work; it just depends whether the comedian is stiff or loose in the neck.

I consider myself a loose-neck comedian. Homework has always scared me and I will always be funnier in the moment than with anything I could prepare. There is normally a correlation between success at school and your approach to comedy. The downside for stiff-neck comedians is that they have to invest so many more hours into developing a show. The downside for loose-neck comedians is that they are constantly living in fear, as they walk out onstage with nothing written down, just faith that something funny will come.

There's a weird grass-is-always-greener relationship between the loosey gooseys and the stiff dicks. Loose necks will dream of having 50 rock-solid one-liners they can reel out, whereas the stiff necks cannot believe that it's possible for someone to walk out onstage and talk and it be instantly funny. Alan Carr, for example, is one of the funniest people I have ever met. I've seen him improvising on stage with the audience eating out of the palm of his hand. He will walk offstage and be exactly the same in the dressing room. Effortlessly funny.

I think your approach to comedy is born out of your formative relationships with school work and preparation. Some people love school, learning and assignments. Some people, like me, just survive school. I have been asked to go back to my secondary school to give a speech to the pupils about how the school helped me achieve my goals. But I can't give the speech because school didn't help me. Not that school specifically, just school in general. I have no issue or problem with the teachers at my secondary school. It was full of good teachers and good people trying their best, but there were simply too many kids and not enough resources for them to do their job. Teaching is one of the hardest and least appreciated jobs in the world. I'm not just saying that to get brownie points from my teacher wife, I mean it. Lockdown and home schooling two kids confirmed that for me. So I have no ill will to the school itself. It's the school system that let them down. I was invisible at that school, a real inbetweener. Not naughty enough to get attention and not intelligent enough to get attention. I was pretty happy with being invisible, too. I just sat there in the middle waiting to be old enough to leave. So here is my speech to anyone who's similar to me at a similar school.

Keep your head down and stay out of trouble.
All the cool kids at 14 will be tragic at 34. Ignore
everything anyone says. Most of the teachers are
going through their own problems. Work hard and

believe in yourself. Higher education is great but not essential. I would recommend it for the social, as most degrees are pointless in the real world. Find something you love to do and work your bollocks off and you'll be all right. If you make loads of money that's a bonus, but if you don't it won't matter because you will enjoy every day at work. Also, there is literally no reason at all to learn algebra and Pythagoras. Coding is the future so make sure you know your way round a computer.

I mean, would a head teacher want a speaker saying that to their school? I went to school in Bromley, which at the time was famous for having one the highest teenage pregnancy rates in the country. When I was 14, I sat between two girls in my maths class who were openly having a discussion about their competition to lose their virginity first. They both went on to become mums before they were 16. Throughout that two-year competition, even though I sat between them, at no point was I in the running to help crown a winner. In their defence I was a very unattractive teenager. I was fat and spotty with tiny spectacles. I looked like the world's youngest paedophile. See the photo in the picture section, if you're brave enough.

A lot of the people I went to school with went on to be self-employed. Lots of builders, gas fitters and plumbers who learned their trade and then set up their own venture. Pretty similar to what I have done, but I chose comedy.

Even though there is an established history of people leaving school at 16 to get an apprenticeship, at no point was there a lesson on how to pay tax or set up a business. It seems mad that we were all forced to learn French but there wasn't even an optional course on how self-assessment tax and VAT work. Don't get me wrong, it's great to have some essential French phrases in my locker like, '*Je puis enlever mon blazer?*' I always struggle with the blistering heat in Calais on a booze cruise, so being able to ask someone if I can take off my blazer is so helpful. You know me, I'm always doing my tax returns in the French sun in my blazer.

All that happened at school in relation to business and money was a sales rep from HSBC – née Midland Bank – turning up and making me sign a form with all my details in exchange for a Filofax and a £5 Our Price voucher. I opened my first bank account for absolutely no reason whatsoever. I was 13 and I had no money. But on the plus side I was never too hot in France. Once I got permission to remove my blazer, I whipped that bad boy off quicker than you could say HMRC.

I don't think hating school is a working-class thing. I think whatever class you are school can be a horrible place. People might think that all your problems are solved if you go to a private school but I don't think that's true. A private education can bring a whole set of other challenges. In the comedy industry I have met hundreds of people who have gone to private schools. From day schools all the way up to world-famous full-boarding schools like Eton and Marlborough College. Most of them hated school just as much as I did.

Being away from your family at boarding school must be so hard. In my experience the working classes regard boarding schools as a form of child abuse. It's a very strange mentality, as normally the working classes can be jealous of middle-class and upper-class families if they can afford more expensive products, like holidays and cars. There are TV shows where working-class people are shown the dream of owning a holiday home, on *A Place in the Sun*, or owning the new Mercedes, on *Top Gear*. Or they are actually physically forced to swap lives with more wealthy or privileged people to show them what they may or may not be missing out on. This show is called *Rich Holiday, Poor Holiday*. That's its actual title. It's the Ronseal of TV class porn.

'What's the show about?'

'Erm, it's about rich holidays and poor holidays.'

'What are we going to call it?'

'*Rich Holidays, Poor Holidays* will do. Keep it simple – it worked for the *News at Ten*.'

The show normally wraps up in a neat conclusion where, actually, the 'poor' people like the budget holiday more than the expensive holiday, which I imagine takes some clever editing and casting to achieve, as I have never known a holiday to get worse the more money you spend on it. That's never happened. Then, as the conclusion develops, the rich people find something quite charming about a budget holiday, normally spouting off some bullshit about simplicity and family time, when the truth is that the rich family will never go back to a budget holiday ever again now that they have had their 15 minutes of fame on Channel 5.

So when it comes to a super-expensive product like a private boarding school education, not only are the working classes not jealous, the actual feeling is one of pity and sorrow tinged with anger towards the upper classes. If I spoke to my mum about a friend sending their daughter to boarding school, her response would be, 'Poor cow, how old is she?' I would reply, 'She's seven,' then my mum would respond with, 'Wicked bastards, sending their kids away. If you don't wanna look after 'em, don't have 'em.' Then my dad would hear from another room and shout, 'I ain't having him come round this house, 'orrible bastard!'

Of course, all families are different and some children respond better to certain situations. But the thought of sending my daughters to a boarding school at the age of seven makes feel sick. I couldn't do it. I would miss them too much. It would be heart-breaking. Is that the normal parental reaction? Or am I a selfish dad who's being too clingy and in reality children need to be independent and take on the world? I don't know the answer to that, but I know that I couldn't cope not seeing my kids every day after school. I even miss them when they are at school during the day. Imagine not seeing your kid for a whole week or term? However, as much as I miss them when they are at school for the day, by about seven minutes past three in the afternoon, when we've already had two meltdowns about fish fingers and *Paw Patrol*, I find myself counting the hours to bath and bed time.

Obviously there are huge benefits to going to a private school, as you get smaller class sizes which enables more one-on-one teaching and pastoral care. But the downside is that the kids who attend private school have a huge expectation to be successful and achieve great things because of the money that has been spent on their education. In some cases they come from so much wealth that the money spent on their education is insignificant. But for a lot of families on a tighter budget they can only just afford to send their kids to private schools. They might sacrifice holidays, new cars and other hobbies in order to pay the school fees. This must put so much pressure on the children, knowing that they need to excel otherwise their parents' money was wasted.

If you don't go to private school there isn't that expectation. I had a great freedom of no expectations growing up. People who have had a private education are always told that they come from great privilege, which is true to an extent. But I experienced the great privilege of having nothing to lose, which allowed me to try new things without worry. If my parents had saved every penny to send me to a private school, I don't think you would be reading this book. I would have been too scared to take any risks.

I never would have tried comedy or a number of other things that I have thrown myself at with a carefree enthusiasm.

I remember when we used to go to restaurants as a family when I was about 11. I would order tap water to save money. A lemonade would cost two or three quid, so I would add it up in my head and think, *If I have three lemonades my dad will have to work longer hours cabbing tomorrow. I would rather have the tap water so he can come home earlier.* This is no reflection on my parents' behaviour – my dad would encourage me to have a fizzy drink and wouldn't care about working longer hours and sometimes wouldn't need to work extra because we had enough money. But in my head I felt like I was forcing my dad to work more by having a £2 lemonade. So the thought of being in an education system that cost my parents £14,000 a year terrifies me. It would have absolutely crushed me in the classroom. I would have felt under so much stress and pressure to perform that I would be consumed with anxiety. Consistently having to achieve high grades and prove that I wasn't wasting my parents' money would be exhausting. On top of that, the worst part would be not being able to complain. Just constantly being told how lucky and privileged you are that you get to go to private school, but inside hating every second of it and being forced into an education system and stereotype that has been picked for you and forced upon you and will define you for ever. Just another

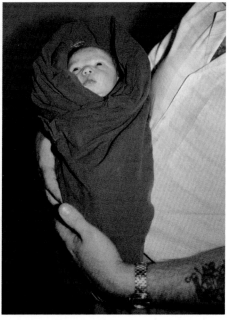

Newborn Bobby Beckett, featuring a lovely gold watch and gold chain combo that got cashed in during the 2008 recession. I think that the economic collapse did my dad a favour in the style stakes.

Mum and Dad back in the day. So happy, and so much hair. Unfortunately the photos were rejected by the Passport Office.

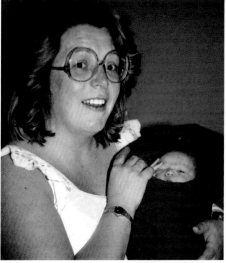

Big glasses from the mum and a big two-fingered 'Fuck you' from the bubba.

Bath time in the Beckett household. Small sink and a big boy!

Here I am in Butlin's in front of an information sign and a bin.

More signage and me as a toddler. It turned out that the pond water level was actually quite low. The pond just kept talking to everyone about its feelings and crying.

Aged five, before my Jaffa nips had fully bloomed.

Just me dressed as Superman cooking up a storm in my kitchen. Let's try to avoid talking about the rug and curtains. Everyone makes bad choices now and again.

Say hello to the world's worst Father Christmas. What shall we do for a snow effect? Hang some bed sheets from the ceiling. Sorted.

The absolute state of those two front teeth. This was about the time the 'Tombstone Teeth' nickname really shifted up a gear.

Me and my brothers in Spain hanging out poolside. I miss that Hulk Hogan T-shirt every single day. What a beauty!

I can't remember if this was a professional awkward family portrait taken in a shopping centre or if we'd been kidnapped and this was on the ransom note – my memory is hazy.

My brother Joe – the human hedgehog – on the left, me on the right trying to do anything I can to contain the teeth.

Taking after my old man. It was either cab driving or the Columbia Road Flower Market.

I'm sixteen in this photo. Being a teenager is fucking horrible.

Britain's youngest paedo.

Me and Dan drinking up the sun on Dymchurch Beach, which is basically a concrete pavement when the tide's in. I'm about fourteen here but look like a fifty-six-year-old car salesman.

The timid hunch of teenage awkwardness. I actually thought I was fat at that age. It's mad the bollocks your thoughts can tell your brain.

The moment my career really took off – Caffé Uno's most focused waiter. I borrowed Gloria Hunniford's hair for my first shift.

The amazing Ross Howat, who rescued me in my time of need in Adelaide.

I went to Australia and all I got was chlamydia from a koala. And look at the state of my barnet . . .

Ross and Catherine Howat's gorgeous family. I can honestly never thank them enough for what they did for me.

The photo on the poster for my first Edinburgh show, *Rob Beckett's Summer Holiday.*

A fishbowl in Spain. Two broken men (me and Lloyd Griffith) from the Edinburgh Fringe reconnecting with their working-class roots the only way they know how.

posh boarding-school kid who had everything handed to him. It sounds absolutely horrific, but I suppose if you end up being a CEO with a place in the sun and the new Mercedes it's all worth it.

But then if you have all the great benefits of a private education with zero pressure or expectations to live up to from parents then it could be a wonderful start in life. I am, of course, only giving you my opinion and how I imagine I would have reacted to a private education, and I'm well aware that I overthink things and suffer with anxiety, so I always place undue pressure on myself. I mean, it's not normal to worry at 11 years of age about the cost of a fucking lemonade in an all-you-can-eat Chinese buffet in Welling, is it? I should add that the irony is not lost on me that I have been spelling privilege incorrectly. Until I got the Word spell checker involved, I had been spelling it 'privelige'.

I think the point I'm getting at is that nobody chooses the hand they are dealt, whether it be a good or bad one, so they shouldn't be judged on it. You can only judge someone on how they play those cards. Growing up, I had an inbuilt suspicion and wariness of the upper classes, but over time I've realised that they aren't all bad. They are just a group of people who know no different to their situation trying to get on with their lives. They are just as fucked up in the head as everybody else. Money and power don't always solve your problems. They resolve some of the big ones but breed new ones to worry about. However much money or power you think you need for your life to be sorted, you will always think you need more.

I also have friends and colleagues who went to Oxford and Cambridge. I still find it so crazy that I move in those circles now. When my daughters get older I'll be able to pick up the phone and ask someone about the application process and advice on the best colleges. Growing up, me and my brothers were the first generation in my family ever to get A levels and go to university. I didn't know anyone who went to university before that. This is not an exaggeration, I mean literally no one. Within one generation the access my children will have to people from different backgrounds has expanded dramatically.

I went to university but I didn't really go to university. I went to Canterbury Christ Church University, which was basically a polytechnic that felt like a slightly jazzed-up, bigger version of sixth form. I 'read' Tourism Management, for literally no other reason than I like holidays and there was a trip to Malta involved. I cannot remember anything from the course – it was a three-year piss-up. I got in with a B in tourism, a D in accounts and an E in law at AS level, not even a full A level! I had about seven UCAS points. But all I knew was that if you went to uni you got a fat loan that didn't need to be paid back as long as you earned under £15,000 a year or moved abroad. So my plan was to rack up a huge student loan debt having the time of my life, then I would either never earn more than £15,000 a year or, if I did, I would emigrate. The reality is that I have paid off all my student debt and my wife's too. I have spent so much money on an education that I have no recollection of. Never has a man paid so much money to learn so little.

I really hated school, both primary and secondary. I found certain academic subjects really hard, almost impossible. As I told you in the introduction, my first parents' evening had a profound effect on me and my education. Being told I was never going to be a high-flyer and that my mum should get some flash cards from the Early Learning Centre was humiliating. I didn't realise how bad that moment was until I went to my five-year-old daughter's school parents' evening and I thought about hearing that from her teacher. Fortunately she said nothing of the sort, as she is a very good teacher, and if you're interested she told me that my kid was doing really well. It dawned on me how brutal and damaging my teacher's words were for me.

I was always incredibly nervous about going to primary school, as believe it or not I struggled with my speech. When I was a toddler no one could understand me. I would speak incredibly quickly, which meant I wasn't enunciating my words properly. I recently asked my mum what my speech was like and she said it sounded like I was speaking Welsh. At the age of three I went to speech therapy for six months and apparently it massively helped. But even now, when I'm excited I speak too quickly and it becomes this relentless stream of ideas, opinions and information. Often if me and Lou are out for dinner with friends or even just having a boring meeting at the bank, Lou will have to squeeze my leg under the table as a cue to slow down, as people can't understand me – and more importantly to let other people speak.

Weirdly, my rapid speech has become a huge asset for me as a comedian. I can get to punchlines quicker and a fast delivery can inject energy into a routine. When I do the voice-over for the E4 dating show *Celebs Go Dating* I can get quick jokes into the tiniest gaps. When I first started narrating the show the producer and editor would say, 'There's no space for a joke in that gap.' I saw it as a challenge and would be able to squeeze it in with an incredibly fast sequence of words.

However, at the age of four I couldn't have realised that my speech impediment would help me get a laugh out of Lee Ryan from Blue eating a burrito in a bowling alley on a date with a call-centre worker called Kerri from Ashby-de-la-Zouch on E4. So as a kid, and sometimes as an adult, I have learned to deal with this lack of confidence in a very specific and brutal way. If I am not instantly good at something I will give up on it and never think about it ever again. For example, algebra, DIY and intercourse. However, if I show an immediate talent for something I will focus on it with an extreme intensity and make sure that I develop that skill to its absolute maximum capacity.

I've been told I'm dyslexic but it's never been officially confirmed or tested. But I do remember being taken off for special-education lessons, where they made me do extra reading to help me catch up with the class. All I can remember is reading a bigger book with the same words, just in a bigger font. It was the same Biff, Chip and Kipper but in Arial font, size 18. I would get told off because I wouldn't read the words; I would look at the pictures and then make up my own stories. The teacher would say that I was doing it wrong, but I thought I was making the story better.

Because there was such little belief in me academically at the start of my education it obliterated any confidence I might have had. It's been 31 years since I was told I would never be a high-flyer and that still upsets me. It makes me feel angry that someone can try to decide the future of a four-year-old. Luckily for me that feedback created a burning desire to prove the teacher wrong, and my parents moved me to another school shortly afterwards. I had a much better time at my new primary school. The teachers were lovely and I made lots of friends, but the wound had already been opened and I did not enjoy the education system. The education system in this country is a one-size-fits-all approach and I, like many others, didn't fit that size.

Everyone always asks, 'What is your earliest memory?' It's so hard to pinpoint. Normally it's your first day of school, a big life event moment. I have flashes of imagery from being small in prams and at nursery. I have an awareness that I was in those places but no searing memory. I find that a memory is super-enhanced or in HD when something physically happens. I have two very clear early memories from when I was about four.

The first is being at a school friend's birthday party. I was a very shy and anxious child, and I remember being overwhelmed because there were all the kids from school at the party and I didn't know them that well because I had only just started at the school. I remember playing with a dinosaur that made a loud 'roar' noise when you pressed a button. I also remember needing a poo desperately but I was too shy to ask where the toilet was. I think you can imagine what I did to solve this problem. Every time I made the dinosaur roar I did some pooing in my pants. The dinosaur was used to cover up any fart noises that might escape – a primitive method that evolved as I got older into running the tap when I had a shit at a new girlfriend's house. The dinosaur-squeeze-push-poo method continued until there had been about nine roars in a row and I was sitting in the middle of a kids' birthday party with a giant shit in my pants. Initially I thought I was a genius and had executed the perfect crime, so it was mortifying when the whole front room smelled of shit and all the kids were looking at me and I realised that my plan had backfired.

It's not really the start you need at school but it does explain why I ended up being a comedian. Let's not beat about the bush here, almost every comedian is unhinged. We are all troubled in some way, some more extreme than others. The nature of the job requires the person involved to crave and need attention and approval from others. Am I driven by the fact that I shit myself in front of my entire class at primary school? Almost definitely. Am I deep down desperately still trying to show everyone I'm not a weirdo? Almost definitely. 'Yes, I did shit myself to the soundtrack of *Jurassic Park*, but I'm no threat – come over here and have a laugh and like me so I feel better about myself!'

One of my favourite things about being a comedian is the backstage green room. No matter how you're feeling or what kind of shit day you're having, you walk in that dressing room and there's another lunatic staring back at you. It makes me feel safe, like an outsider union – a sense of weirdo strength in numbers. I love being a part of it. When I do the comedy clubs and open-mic spots turn up for their first gig, I look in their eyes and know as soon as they open their mouth if they have what it takes to be a comedian. Being funny isn't enough; you need a drive and determination that can't be manufactured. You just get a feeling when you know you're looking at one of your own.

It's also a complete level playing field when you are onstage. Obviously class, race and gender can stop or help you getting onto that stage, but once you're on it's a brutally exposing experience. You either make them laugh or you don't. It's not like any other art form, where the audience reaction can be interpreted in a number of ways. Comedy's beauty is its simplicity: they laugh and you win; they don't laugh and you lose. Even the language used to describe comedy is dramatic. You either kill it or you die. No excuses.

The second earliest vivid memory I have is of being at school in a music lesson. Now, I am tone deaf, have no rhythm, can't play an instrument and don't understand how singing works. When I try to sing I just talk faster and louder with music in the background. However, I didn't know any of this when I was four and walking into my first music lesson full of excitement. We were learning to play the recorder, and the instruments were in a big bucket of water, which I think was to be hygienic but looking back feels like some sort of Covid bucket of spit and saliva hell. The bucket was rammed with recorders, and once we all took an instrument the bucket was left empty, apart from the disgusting water.

We started to play the recorders under instruction from the teacher. I was trying my best, as I like to do things right. I love to know if I am doing something right, which I think is another reason why I love stand-up comedy so much. So I was smashing out 'Three Blind Mice' on this recorder as best I could, giving it the full welly treatment because when I do something I do it properly. I wasn't just playing 'Three Blind Mice' with 40 other kids at a primary school – I was onstage at Wembley playing for my life. I was playing like someone had my family hostage and the only way they would release them safely was if I got a standing ovation and an encore.

So, as I was playing the teacher came over to speak to me, and I was thinking, *I am nailing this. Here comes the teacher to give me some praise. Am I going to get a star sticker? Will I get a mention in assembly? Or, even better, has Simon Cowell been on the blower? He must have heard about this recorder-playing child prodigy and he wants me for* Britain's Got Talent?

Unfortunately none of these things transpired. What actually happened was even more unexpected. The teacher removed me from the group and sent me out of the classroom because she thought I was being bad at the recorder on purpose. This was heart-breaking for me, as I was genuinely trying the best I could. I was so upset that I cried and tried to explain that I wasn't being bad on purpose. To this day it's the worst review I have ever received. How badly must I have been playing for the teacher to think I was being shit on purpose? I was just shit and enthusiastic.

So my most vivid earliest memory is me putting my recorder back in the big empty bucket of water. All I could think was how weird one lonely recorder looked in that big bucket. I stood outside the class distraught, one lonely boy in a big school corridor thinking about his performance of 'Three Blind Mice'. I look back at that moment and wonder what would have happened to me if I'd had a better education. Not necessarily a private education, just a better school. A comprehensive in the countryside where it was a lot calmer, with smaller class sizes. Would I still have become a comedian? Would I still have a mad work ethic powered from a part of my brain that wanted to prove people wrong? I'm not so sure. I think I would have had more self-confidence and I would know my own worth, though.

I left school feeling worthless. From primary school until I left school at 18, I hid away waiting for it to finish. I couldn't wait to leave school and my local area. Maybe with better pastoral care someone at the school might have helped me come out of my shell. But with 35 kids in a classroom it's easy to hide. Again, this is just my experience of school. I know plenty of kids who went to the same schools as me and had a good time and have done really well for themselves. My daughters also love going to school and preschool, to the point that I'm standing there in disbelief watching them skip into school.

I never did drama or any performances at my school, which seems absolutely mad now, considering my career. The first time I stood on stage was at the age of 23, to do my first gig. I was fucking shit, even though I tried my best, so my music teacher might have been onto something. But the difference was that I didn't put my microphone back in a big bucket of water. For some reason I can't explain, I kept going back onstage, and even though I was crap at the start I grafted and learned to get better and better. It was a slog but it paid off.

EDUCATION

The normal response me and my mates from school would give about a private education is, 'What's the point of private school? Going to a comprehensive in South East London didn't do me no harm.' Which is true. But it didn't do me much good, either. However, if I had gone to Eton and been offered a broker internship in the City for decent money, would I still have put that effort into comedy? The answer is almost definitely not. So for me, I'm still not sure how helpful or damaging it was to be told I'd never be a high-flyer. I'm starting to realise that it might have been the best thing that happened to me. It was like they poured petrol on a bonfire. And, truth be told, who wants to be good at the recorder? It's the second-shittest instrument going, just behind the triangle.

THE ARTS AND CULTURE

Things I did before I started writing this chapter

••••••••••••••••••••••••••••

NOTHING – I AM ACTUALLY REALLY
ENJOYING WRITING IT; I DIDN'T THINK
THAT WOULD HAPPEN

••••••••••••••••••••••••••••

I think ignorance is bliss would best sum up my early career in comedy. I didn't even know BBC Radio 4 existed until I was asked to be on it as a guest on a comedy panel show, and even then I thought it was one of the new BBC digital stations that launched in 2002, like Radio 6 Music and Radio 1Xtra. For some of my peers in the comedy industry it was a massive deal. The pressure on them to perform was huge, as all of their family were at home listening. I didn't even bother telling anyone I was on it. No one I knew would care or know what I was talking about. I was oblivious that Radio 4 was this hugely important part of British comedy. But the truth is that it isn't really an important part of British comedy for a big portion of the country. Of course it is loved across the UK and has produced some amazing shows over the years, but mainly for a middle- and upper-class audience. I have never been in the pub and had someone say to me, 'I listened to a great radio comedy the other day.' But then maybe I'm in the minority and people are having these conversations. I've just never been a part of it, so for me in that bubble it feels alien.

I used to feel a bit embarrassed about it at times. When I went on *The Chris Evans Breakfast Show* on Radio 2 to do some promotion for my tour, I had to prerecord something for the show in a separate studio before I went live on air. I plonked myself down in a chair in front of the mic and the producer said, 'Oooh, this must be exciting – you get to sit in Ken Bruce's chair.' Now, at that point I had no fucking idea who Ken Bruce was. For some reason I thought he might have been an actor from *Neighbours*. Ken Bruce just sounds like an Australian. So I politely said, 'My mum and dad are going to be so excited.'

For a few years this was my stock response when I needed to be excited about something that I was clueless about. Mainly because I had heard posh boys say this kind of thing. The reality was that my mum would be totally nonplussed about her son sitting in Ken Bruce's chair. This is not a dig at Ken Bruce, who is a wonderful man and a broadcasting legend. I had the pleasure of appearing on his show, and it was great fun and he couldn't have been nicer.

One thing that surprised me about the Radio 2 *Breakfast Show* was that at one point, straight after the news and traffic, there was a religious bit. Normally a Christian gives a quick shout out to God, local community and forgiveness. I didn't know this was going to happen, and religion always scares me. I'm not religious at all – not because I'm against it, I just don't know anything about it or where to start. Religion is like veganism. It's probably the right thing to do but there's a lot of faff involved. I live in a house with three women, which has its challenges, so the last thing I need is the Big Man upstairs telling me what to do on top of my family.

I didn't know that when the religious bit of the show started, it was essentially 'banter off' time for the guests on the show. So as the Christian person (is that the right label? He could have been a vicar but he was in casual clothes, like it was dress-down Friday) began to talk, I started chipping in, having a laugh like I was on *Mock the Week*. Stuff like, 'All right, captain sensible. Calm down, mate, we're trying to have a laugh and listen to Deacon Blue. It's 7 a.m., why are we chatting about sins and forgiveness? My morning coffee hasn't kicked in yet.' As soon as I said it I knew I'd misjudged this bit of banter live on air to six million people. I got a death stare from the producer but out of the corner of my eye I could see the other guest on the show laughing to himself. It was one of my heroes, Liam Gallagher. So what started as one of the worst moments of my career immediately switched into a highlight. I could honestly say, 'My mum and dad are going to be so excited,' and mean it.

It's such a strange feeling to be in a world you know nothing about and constantly have to pretend you do so you can fit in. It's a constant blag, which I think is why working-class people in the media suffer from imposter syndrome. Sometimes the truth of it is that being able to make people laugh thrusts you into a world you know nothing about and know no one in it. The same way being able to sing, dance and act enables you to jump a few levels without the need for networking or family ties. TV and radio is a huge industry created mostly by powerful middle-class white men, which is why some talented working-class acts can slip into the cruise-ship/holiday-camp circuit, as it feels like a safer and more comfortable environment.

It must be even harder for black and Asian acts to try to fit into that white middle-class world, which is why I think the urban live comedy circuit is of such a high quality and there isn't enough diversity on screen. It's a daunting prospect to enter such a strange and alien world when the live comedy circuit is well paid and the crowd love and adore you. It must be so difficult to try to push into the mainstream media when someone so different to you is trying to produce you and mould you into what they think is representative of your race or culture.

I remember the first time I did *Mock the Week*, which in the past has been known as a tough and intimidating TV panel show. On the circuit you would be told it was impossible to get a joke in and the panel didn't welcome new comedians with open arms. Mainly because when *Mock the Week* first started there weren't many TV opportunities for comedians, so anyone who was a regular on the show did not want to lose their spot, as being a regular meant you could start to tour the UK and move on from the club circuit. Competition on the show was fierce, especially during the Frankie Boyle and Russell Howard era, in part to do with their boisterous and confident delivery, but mainly due to the fact that they are both really funny and it's hard to compete with people who are so talented.

The atmosphere on *Mock the Week* now is much more calm and welcoming, which I think has changed alongside the increase in opportunities for comics on TV and online. If you don't get booked or rebooked on *Mock the Week* in 2021 it's not the end of the world, as there are other avenues for exposure to build a fan base. I started doing *Mock the Week* after Frankie and Russell had left, but it was still very competitive. People warned me that I would be intimidated and scared and that it was so ruthless. I was petrified, but what I realised was that it was intimidating mostly to overly polite middle-class people. When I was told it was scary, I was expecting 6-foot-7 Dara Ó Briain to corner me and say, 'If you talk over me on this show I will break your fucking jaw and you won't gig for six months.' But that didn't happen at all. Dara is one of the nicest and most welcoming people you will meet. Sure, during the recording it's a bit of a scramble to get jokes out and the nature of the show means people occasionally talk over each other, but that's not intimidating – that's just loud.

For those not familiar with the show, in the final round, Scenes I Would Like to See, all the comics stand on a step and when a topic is selected you walk to the microphone to tell your joke. There is no order, just first come, first served, and sometimes it's frustrating if someone walks really fast to the microphone and you miss your opportunity. As a 5-foot-8 man I found it very hard to keep up with the massive leg strides of 6-foot-plus Hugh Dennis and Chris Addison. I had to be quick off the mark to get to the mic first. Poor old 5-foot-3 Josh Widdicombe has to employ a superspeed little-leg shuffle to get to the mic in time. Ultimately everyone is on the show trying their best to be as funny as possible. It's a stressful and nerve-racking environment, but no one is trying to be mean or difficult.

I will happily accept competitiveness and being spoken over. As long as I come out of it physically unharmed, I will take that as a win. Plus, when you've grown up in a family of five boys and a huge extended family you are used to being shouted down and ignored. I've found trying to get an anecdote out at Christmas dinner with my family much more difficult than getting a joke in on *Mock the Week*. In one particularly low moment of scene-stealing attention-seeking I once attempted to down a two-litre bottle of water in one go to stop the dinner table conversation and divert the eyes back onto me.

My wife always tells me I am too loud in public but I think I'm just a product of my environment. In the battle to be heard in a family of five boys I've been punched in the leg and had my mouth smothered in my family home so a sibling can get a story out at the dinner table. I have been both perpetrator and victim of these silencing attacks in my time. This conversation-dominance-through-violence strategy that was required growing up really helped me build a bulletproof armour when it came to group discussion, which means I can handle a passive-aggressive eye-roll off a middle-aged bloke in terrible clothes on a panel show.

Now, don't get me wrong, I'm not trying to say I've always done brilliantly on panel shows. I have died on my arse on a number of occasions and been saved by the edit, but it never knocked my confidence or stopped me from trying. I was almost oblivious to a joke dying. I would just plough on regardless. Whether that's an upbringing thing or the naivety of youth, either way it helped. I've always had it in my head that if I think a joke is funny that's enough. If the crowd don't like it that's up to them, and if at the next few gigs those crowds don't laugh I'll probably drop the joke. But in the moment I'm not going to dwell on it not working; I'm going push on with the next one.

Someone I did find intimidating on TV was Sean Lock, mainly because he was so good. He was the don of panel shows. I don't think anyone came close to him. He constantly delivered brilliant jokes and surreal ideas that were always funny. I loved watching him as a kid, so when I got to appear on *8 Out of 10 Cats*, for me it was like playing up front for Arsenal with Dennis Bergkamp.

The reasons why Sean Lock was so intimidating to work with were threefold. First of all, he was a genius, so you were always slightly in awe of him when he performed on the show. Secondly, he didn't suffer fools gladly. He had such high standards for himself and he expected the same from guests appearing on the show, so if you weren't delivering at the level required you knew about it, mainly from the slightly disappointed glare you'd receive from him. I imagine the same kind of glare Dennis Bergkamp would give Glenn Helder if he misplaced a pass to the non-flying Dutchman. Thirdly, Sean was very old-school working class and had the air of a man who would have a fight in the street if he deemed it necessary. I don't know if that was true, as I never saw Sean Lock even nearly have a fight. But my working-class spider senses kicked into overdrive around Sean. He had the presence of a man who could have a tear-up. It was much more intimidating trying to tell decent jokes while sitting next to a man who could beat the shit out of you if he'd wanted.

It was an honour and privilege to have worked with Sean. As well as being one of the most gifted and unique comedy minds of a generation, he was a good man who loved his family more than anything. Even though he was only here for 58 years he managed to pack in hundreds of years of funny into that time and, luckily for us, we have YouTube, so we can watch and enjoy his comedy forever.

I was petrified the first time I did *8 Out of 10 Cats*. I didn't speak for ages. I just sat there thinking, *This is great, I have got such good seats to watch this show.* Then my brain woke up and was like, *Fucking hell, Rob, you're not watching it, you're on it!* I had never been to see a TV show recorded before, and now I was on the show. I remember Jon Richardson was so nice to me before the show. He is one of the most genuine and caring people I have ever met. He could obviously tell I was nervous so he asked me if I had any jokes in particular I wanted to say that he could set me up for. It's a topical news show so you're supposed to write jokes about the week's news. I panicked and did all my jokes from my comedy club set, but he was so nice and reassuring and helped me have a good show.

Jon is from a working-class background and there was a definite acknowledgement of that when we first worked together. There were also lots of middle-class people who were lovely to me when I first started working in TV. But it was always a different interaction with working-class people on TV sets. Like an unspoken union that we had fluked it into this position so let's look out for each other so we can stay for as long as we can.

It was the same interaction with Paddy McGuiness when I first met him. I will never forget how lovely he was to me. I was doing the audience warm-up for a panel show he was on. TV audience warm-up is one of the hardest jobs in entertainment. Your job is to chat to the audience and get them pumped up for the show. Mark Olver, Stuart Holdham, Andy Collins, Karl Lucas, Andrew Bird and James Gill are all excellent at it, but it's a really tough job. The audience are there for the show and not the warm-up act, so you are almost stopping the audience from getting what they want.

I was not a good warm-up act. I had no idea what I was doing. I was very new and, in what was becoming my calling card, I just performed my comedy club set at them. Stuff like, Why is pitta bread so hot when it comes out of the toaster? Or other gold-dust routines about why I didn't trust couscous. The answer? Because it feels like it's already been chewed. 'It's fat sand!' I used to shout to finish my routine. So I was dying on my arse hard and the audience could not have been less warm. I am talking tepid at best, other side of the pillow cool. When you are a shit warm-up act people in the studio leave you alone like you're patient zero of Covid-20. Forget the onscreen famous people, even the producers and camera crew ignore you. It was like being shit at my job was contagious and they didn't want to catch it. But I vividly remember Paddy McGuiness coming up to me and being so supportive. Unfortunately he did catch being shit at his job from me, but it's not held him back. I'm obviously joking – Paddy is one of the best TV presenters in the country.

He was so kind to me that day, telling me that I had great material and the audience were just a bad crowd that day. All the clichés you tell someone who's been shit at their job. But I think he saw a working-class bloke trying his best and learning on the job. His encouragement really helped me and gave me a confidence boost that helped me get through it. I try my very best now to help and support other young performers coming through. Sometimes you're so busy and stressed with your own job that you forget to, but it's something I always try to do.

I sometimes think that if I hadn't had people like Paddy and Jon praising me and offering supportive words I might not have carried on with comedy. There have definitely been moments when I've thought about quitting. One of those was when I performed at the gala dinner of a huge banking conference. It was the worst death I have ever had onstage. The gig was in the ballroom of a five-star hotel in front of a thousand bankers, all on million-pound salaries and dressed in black tie. I was about 24 and all of my material was about being working class. I was wearing a black suit from George at Asda that cost about £35. The material was so cheap that when I walked and the tops of my thighs rubbed together, I was worried my crotch was going to catch on fire.

It has to go down as one of the worst booking decisions of all time. Worse than booking Matt Hancock to host the *GQ* Men of the Year Awards. I walked out onstage full of hope and ambition. For the first five minutes all of my jokes were ignored or jeered. At one point, trying desperately to get into a routine about Barcelona, I said, 'Has anyone here been to Barcelona?' Someone heckled back, 'I commute from Barcelona.' This was definitely not my crowd and I was too new and inexperienced to deal with it.

I still had 15 minutes to go in what was no longer a gig. I felt like the mayor of a small town that I had made bankrupt through fraud. The townspeople were furious with me, but I couldn't leave the stage before I had completed my contractually obliged 20 minutes. About halfway through the show/public humiliation, one of the bankers was so sick of me that he stood up and said, 'If I give you £1,000 will you fuck off the stage and leave us alone?' This being a middle-aged, rich, alpha-male audience, it meant a ferocious and surreal bidding war followed.

One of them chipped in with, 'I'll give you two grand to fuck off.'

This carried on and escalated to the point that I was running an auction to see how much a banker would pay for me to 'fuck off'. I got them up to ten grand, which was astronomically more than I was getting paid, so I said, 'Deal. If you give me ten grand I will fuck off immediately.'

'But you've got to give the ten grand to charity,' the winning bidder said.

'Absolutely no chance,' I said. 'I'm getting paid tonight. I'm going to finish my set.'

Now, I don't want to look uncharitable, but I couldn't afford to give up my fee that night. I needed to pay my rent so I limped through the last five minutes as they chanted, 'Off! Off! Off! Off! Off!' Just before I put the mic in the stand and left the stage I may or may not have called them all a bunch of stuck-up twats. I can't quite recall, my memory is hazy. As I left the stage I was exhausted and upset and desperate to get back home and wondering if I should jack it all in. Just as I was leaving the hotel the event organiser ran up to me and said, 'Where are you going?'

I said, 'To a very dark place with a pizza and three bottles of wine.'

She said, 'You can't. You've got to host the awards.'

I couldn't fucking believe it. I thought I was only doing some stand-up. There must have been a mix-up or an email I missed, but either way I had no choice. I was back out in front of the mob to host their shitting banking awards. The ironic cheers and applause I received when I walked out on that stage again were deafening. They were loving it. 'He's come back for more,' and, 'Encore!' were being shouted at me from all over the ballroom.

As I walked up to the lectern to thunderous sarcastic applause I could hear Alan Dedicoat, the *Strictly* and National Lottery voiceover man, who was announcing the award nominees and winners, on the PA system. He's not just big money balls and foxtrots – he does banking gigs too. 'Back by indifferent demand,' he announced, 'it's your host, Mr Rob Beckett … Don't worry, Rob, we have the car running. This is one for the autobiography. You've earned your money tonight.' He wasn't wrong and I had to laugh.

I reached a point in my career when I had performed in more West End theatres than I had attended as an audience member. Theatre was not really on our radar as a family, and even if it had been, it was far too expensive to go regularly. As a kid we did go to some shows – I remember going to see *The Buddy Holly Story* and *Mamma Mia!* at the theatre and I loved it. My dad would pick us up right outside the venue in his black cab and take us home. There were always too many people for the cab so the adults and older kids would sit in the back and the smallest would go in the footwell next to the driver. Which at the time felt so exciting but it petrifies me now.

The best thing about having a dad as a black cab driver was the free journeys home from London. When I first started gigging he would pick me up from comedy clubs and drive me home. That was an absolute touch. Of course, he would always put the meter on to show me how much it would have cost, but he never charged me. He just wanted to let me know how much I was costing him. I would wind him up, saying, 'You wouldn't need to earn so much if you didn't have so many kids. No one forced you to have five kids.'

The only rule with the free cab home was that he would keep his light on, and if someone hailed him in the street and wanted to be taken to Heathrow Airport then I would have to get out of the cab and make my own way home. This never happened but I would have been cool with it. You cannot deprive a black cab driver a Heathrow job. That's the zenith of London cabbing.

When I was young, I would hear my mum on the phone to my dad, and she would relay the news to us that Dad had got two airport jobs so he might be home early that night. We would cheer in the front room. No one loved hearing the words 'Dad's got a Heathrow' more than us. We would be allowed to stay up late to see my dad come home from work. I have vivid memories of running out into the cold night, barefoot, to see my dad park up the cab round the back of the house. He would come in with wads of cash that me and my brothers would count for him and my mum would take care of.

The mum is the don of a working-class house. The dads are the foot soldiers and enforcers. They might look like they're in charge but they work for a big boss. My dad would tentatively let himself in and, while still holding his work bag, shuffle into the darkened front room that would be filled with cigar smoke. He would be presented with the intimidating silhouette of Big Suze. She would ask how much he had earned and decide if he was allowed in for the night. If he had enough cash she would give him a nod and he would put his bag down and relax.

My dad didn't just use the footwell of his taxi to transport children – he made temporary seating in the family car too. I don't know if it's a class thing, a 1990s thing or just a Beckett thing, but it was definitely a thing. We didn't have a seven-seater when we were kids, but we had a Renault estate car and my dad would make a bench seat in the boot out of two suitcases that me and my brother would sit on with no seatbelts. Then we would drive for hours on motorways to Devon or Great Yarmouth for a holiday. At the time it felt like the most exciting thing in the world. We were completely oblivious as to how dangerous and illegal it was.

If I set up suitcase seats now for my daughters I think they would report me to the police themselves. However, I think car-seat safety might have gone a bit overboard since I was younger. The set-up for children in 2021 is an absolute joke. I'm pretty sure that the Isofix seat was invented by NASA for space travel. The seats are insanely heavy. Too heavy for grandparents to move. So when they come to collect their grandchildren, who I have been babysitting for them, I have to put the car seats in their car for them. It's like doing the Atlas Stones in *World's Strongest Man*. After the seat transfer I have an ice bath and begin two days of recovery before I have to babysit my parents' grandchildren again.

You get a slightly lighter car-seat option at the age of four. Still an Isofix, but less heavy. The car seat I purchased for my then four-year-old will apparently fit them until they are twelve years of age. Surely that's too old for a car seat – that's Year 8 of secondary school. Someone born later in the year could potentially be cruising up to school for their Year 9 SATs in a fucking car seat. That can't be acceptable. Of course it's a car safety issue, but what about school playground safety? How is a kid expected to be safe from bullies when they are still in a child's car seat at twelve? Some kids are early developers. Imagine having pubes and still being strapped into your car seat for the school run. Or getting a whiff of your son's BO as you lean over their massive hairy chest and strap them into the Isofix.

I think my limited experience of theatres helped me out in my early career. I found it easier to perform at the London Palladium and other such venues because I had never been there to watch a show. I was mostly oblivious to the history of the venue and how important it was to British entertainment. My experience of the Palladium was the stage door then a corridor then a bit of curtain then the stage and a sea of darkness. It felt like any other gig. It was only after I'd performed and I went to see my parents in the audience that I started to get nervous. I managed to get stage fright after I had been on stage. From the stalls it's so big and posh and daunting. There's gold everywhere and big red seats. I remember sitting with them for a quick chat, asking how my set went and if they were enjoying themselves. As I walked off backstage my brain started whirring, saying, *Oooh, Rob, that looks a bit scary. I wouldn't fancy doing that show, that doesn't look like a gig for you.* I was thinking to myself, *What are you talking about? We've just done it.*

I weirdly talk to myself in my own head and sometimes out loud. I am aware that I am not normal and my wife often reminds me too. I'm not unusual in a 'I'm a performer, you wouldn't understand' drama-school kind of way. I'm a lunatic. I laugh out loud in my sleep all the time. When I feel down, I will try to think of a situation that would be fun and exciting. But not for me – for the person I have invented in my head. It's almost like lucid dreaming when I'm awake. So, for example, I will close my eyes and imagine that I am someone who runs a business that makes and supplies cardboard boxes. In this daydream that person will be at a party and he gets introduced to Jeff Bezos. Now, it's exciting enough to be introduced to the world's richest man, but not only is he insanely successful, he owns Amazon. Which means he surely needs more cardboard boxes than anyone else in the world. Now, imagine the surge of energy, excitement and adrenalin your imaginary character is feeling right now. It's bubbling up in their veins. You sell boxes and he buys boxes. To think you nearly didn't come to this party. So, in my head I will try to recreate that moment of electricity when imaginary cardboard-maker man leans into Bezos over the buffet in between mouthfuls of vol-au-vents and says, 'Bezos, who does your boxes?' I told my wife this and she said I was a strange little man and no one else thinks like that.

At the age of 5 my daughter has been to as many theatre shows as I had by the age of 25. That has a lot to do with my wife, who is obsessed with musical theatre and the West End. On one of our first dates we went to see the play *War Horse* and no one really explained to me the interval drinks system. I thought it was just laid out like a buffet and you could help yourself. I couldn't imagine a world where people would have that much trust to pay for a drink and then expect the drink to get left out on the side and not drunk. This was not the only thing that confused me and still to this day makes me angry. There was also the posh fake laughter in a theatre. In a serious play it's so easy to get a laugh. It's because everything in it is so serious and intense that any humour really cuts through. I can't stand it. I always lean over to Lou and say, 'That would never get a laugh in a stand-up show,' and she tells me to shut up.

The worst unearned laugh appeared in *War Horse* during a bit when all the dialogue was in French, which for most people means you sit there in silence with no idea what is going on, praying for them to switch back into English. All I could hope for was a horse that was too hot wearing a blazer so I could keep up with the plot. Unfortunately for me there was no sweaty-betty blazer-wearing equine. But then in the Gallic silence one person, a big red-faced alcoholic in training, laughed out loud, basically to subtly tell everyone that he knew French and we single-language plebs had missed an absolute zinger of a punchline. This guy was laughing so hard I thought he was going to unclog his arteries. Now, I know the anger I'm feeling comes from a defensive part of me that feels inferior because I can't speak French, but surely the joke wasn't funny enough for that reaction. Let's remember that this play is about a horse that dies in a war. It's hardly *Carry on Camping*, is it?

I have taken my parents to the West End for birthdays and Christmas presents. They love it but some would argue that they love it too much. We went to see *Sunny Afternoon*, the musical about the Kinks. This is a nice entry level to the West End for working-class people. It's in a posh theatre but it's got songs we already know from *Top of the Pops*. My dad loves the Kinks and loved the musical so much that he sang along. That's right, my dad sang out loud during a musical. Even I know that is not acceptable, and the tutting and staring from the other theatre-goers confirmed it. And while I found it awkward, it made Lou want to curl up and die.

I still feel out of place in theatres. I think comedians in general always feel like outsiders. You have to be an outsider to observe the world and then write jokes about what you see. Plus, I've always felt like comedy is the necessary evil of the arts, and that theatres to a point have to put up with us comedians. Let's face it, most theatre directors deep down want to put on opera, ballet and Shakespeare plays, as it's seen as classy and earns respect. No theatre director is boasting to their friends that they had me at their venue doing dick jokes for an hour and a half. But comedy sells lots of tickets and comedy audiences drink a lot and spend loads at the bar, so it's a win-win for the venue.

What's strange is that I only feel out of place in a theatre when it's empty. Once the audience arrive I feel comfortable and relaxed, especially on tour, when it's my audience. It's like your mates arriving for backup. Sometimes the aesthetic of a historic old theatre gets too much respect and admiration. People will say, 'Isn't it a wonderful venue? Look how beautiful it is.' But the truth is that without the audience it's nothing. The audience make the venue come alive. I don't care how red and velvety the seats are or how much gold leaf there is. The décor has never helped me out by laughing when I'm having a tough gig. So am I comfortable in the middle class world of the arts? Well, I still don't know what stage right and stage left are. No one has ever told me and it seems ridiculous to ask at this stage. But yes, I do now feel comfortable in theatres. Just as long as 2,000 working-class people invade that venue and occupy it for two hours, I feel like a big, smiley, comfortable pig in shit.

HOME

London is such a weird place to come from. It's so huge, it's almost five cities in one place. The first major issue is the north–south divide, where people from North London feel uncomfortable south of the river and vice versa. It's not just a joke, either. I have travelled all over the world and nothing matches that feeling of relief arriving home to safety as you come through the Blackwall Tunnel southbound and see the 02 arena and that dodgy nightclub right next to the tunnel. It's a weird sensation and I think I know why it exists. The problem with North London to a South Londoner is that North London looks exactly the same as South London, but you don't know anyone or where anything is. There's a strange feeling of familiarity with a lonely confusion.

Even though I am a Londoner I find it mind-blowing that people actually live in central London. You see all those massive Mary Poppins houses that are worth about £8 million. I find myself walking around places like Covent Garden and Mayfair thinking, *How do you ever afford a house like that?*

I remember walking through Mayfair on my way to a meeting. I had a look in a charity shop window and saw a second-hand Gucci jumper on sale for £300. I have never been so shocked in my life. I had so many questions. Who's spending £300 on something second-hand? Who's giving away Gucci jumpers? How much did it cost originally in the shop? I think about that jumper once a week. Is it still there? Or did it get sold? If so, where is it now? Surely it will end up in a cycle of charity shops forever. No one would ever throw away a Gucci jumper, would they?

Growing up, fashion played a big part of my adolescence. Lads from South East London take a lot of pride in what they wear and how they look. Bromley, where I went to school, is a bit like Essex but less flash and more fights. I once saw two 18-year-olds in Zara in Bromley trying on suit jackets to wear, I imagined, to the Queen's Head in Chislehurst before going to the Venue in New Cross. The ultimate night out, growing up. One of the boys had the jacket on and his mate asked him how it fit and then if he could throw a punch in it. What proceeded was a full shadowboxing display by a lad in a light-grey double-breasted suit jacket. He was actually checking to see if he could have a fight in his jacket without ripping it. No one in the shop battered an eyelid. Unintentional pun, but a good one, so I will keep it in.

I'm not sure if it's a class thing or just a South East London thing, but parents round my way dress their kids so old. You will see a 30-year-old bloke in a Ralph Lauren polo shirt tucked into tailored shorts with a leather belt and metal buckle, combined with a pair of brown loafers and gelled hair. He will be standing next to his three-year-old son wearing the exact same outfit. Now, I don't know if it's because the parents want them to dress like that or the kids want to look like their parents.

I remember when we were expecting our first baby I was in America for work. Which for a working-class kid from London means one thing and one thing only: Ralph Lauren outlet store. Ralph Lauren is the aspirational uniform of choice for the working classes. I don't know anyone from my area who doesn't have at least one item of Ralph Lauren. It's so weird that an American brand that features a man on horseback playing polo has almost become a symbol of working-class Britain.

The thing is, Ralph Lauren is expensive in the UK, so having Ralph Lauren clothes is a sign of success and prestige. But the American Ralph Lauren outlet stores are a shortcut to that prestige. Sure, you have to pay for a flight to America, but Ralph Lauren is so much cheaper over there. People would come back head to toe in 'Ralph', as it's known for short. So when I was out there I bought loads of clothes for my unborn daughter. I was so excited to show Lou the bargains I had found, taking her through all the outfits and googling the price in the UK then showing her the lower dollar price on the label.

Lou was polite but not overly enthused, and I thought nothing more of it. It was only about a year later when I realised that all those clothes were still in the wardrobe, barely worn. So I asked what had happened to the clothes and she came clean. I said, 'You hate the Ralph clothes, don't you?' She said she didn't hate the clothes, she just didn't use them. The truth is that she did hate the clothes but I was so excited that she didn't have the heart to tell me. She had dressed the baby in the plain Ralph basics but none of the, let's be frank, 'formal' dresses. I said, 'Why didn't you like the dresses?' She said they were too grown up for our cute little baby. She had put one of the dresses on her and she said our four-month-old baby looked like a 56-year-old millionairess divorcee from Florida. I looked at the photo and had to agree. She looked like the kind of proud US citizen that would play a round of golf in Mexico while sipping on a Corona and wearing a 'Make America Great Again' cap.

The dream for most kids round my way was a gold Rolex and a Range Rover. If you had that you had truly made it. My favourite thing to see is 18-year-old lads with a Rolex and a Range Rover parked outside their parents' house, where they still live. I'm a big fan of observing people with their priorities in the complete wrong order. It's a weird phenomenon, but being perceived to have made it is more important than actually making it in my area. The truth of it is that the people with the most money look like they have the least. Trust me, go to a top hotel like the Ritz and there will be people from working-class and middle-class backgrounds having afternoon tea in suits and dresses, all dolled up for their big day out. But at reception there's always a fat, slobby bloke in sliders and misshapen jogging bottoms who's staying in a suite for three weeks. The super-rich do not give a shit.

The drop off between the richest and poorest in London is staggering. It feels like the super-rich live in their own London bubble that normal Londoners are excluded from. There is a posh mega-mansion road in central London that actually closes at 11 p.m. to car traffic. I used to use it all the time when I drove back late from gigs up north. I would cut through the whole of London at 1 a.m. because there was no traffic. Then one week the road was closed to traffic. There was no explanation at all, no roadworks or anything like that. It felt like the people who lived there either paid for a barrier or they had connections with the council or Transport for London and asked them to shut the road at night because of the noise. I have no idea if this is true but it's the only reason I can think of. I wasn't the only person using this cut-through so the noise must have been fairly loud. But as someone who lived on the New Cross one-way system for four years I have little sympathy.

Our flat in New Cross was in the middle of four busy roads, Goldsmiths University, New Cross station, Millwall pubs and the Venue nightclub. It must be one of the loudest places on earth to live. On top of that our neighbour was a drug dealer so would have customers knocking 24/7 on the front door of the flats. Luckily they only dealt weed, so it was quite a calm, slow, lethargic knock at the door. Must be a nightmare living next door to a coke dealer. To give you a clearer idea of how busy an area we were living in, the road outside our front door had three lanes of traffic *and* a double-red no-parking line on it. Now, that is an intense parking restriction. It doesn't get much more serious than the double red. If you park on a single yellow line you get a fine and then it escalates through to double yellow, then single red, until you arrive at our doorstep on double trouble. I think if you are caught parking on a double-red line it's an instant six-month prison sentence with a lashing. I think it's one lash per minute parked on a double red. The only crime levels above the double red are parking on a zig-zag outside a school and first-degree murder.

So I was used to a busy loud road and fully aware that if I did complain, the council would not just shut the road. I need to make it clear that I have no idea if this is what the big, posh mansion-road committee did. I have also invented this committee in my head – I don't know if that exists either. But when a road is closed which adds 15 minutes onto your journey when it's already 1 a.m., the working-class chip on your shoulder comes out to play.

I was sitting in my 25-year-old Volkswagen Golf, talking to myself under my breath. Stuff like, 'Cheeky rich bastards, sitting there in their massive fucking houses. I'm trying to make something of myself. I'm skint as shit and they won't even let me drive through their road at night in case I wake them up.' In this tired and emotional state I did what any normal, well-balanced person would do. I drove home safely and sensibly and got a good night's sleep because tomorrow was a new day.

But we all know that isn't what happened. This is what happened. I drove onto the pavement to get around the barrier then I wound down my window (I know, not even electric windows – poor me). I proceeded to drive at milk-float speed, beeping my horn constantly down the mega-posh mansion road, screaming at the top of my voice, 'Wakie, wakie, you rich bastards!'

Now, after this manic working-class hero, Wolfie Smith tribute act, did I feel any better? Or was it the pathetic cry for help of an emotionally weak man with nothing? Well, it was definitely the act of a pathetic man, but it did make me feel better. If I am brutally honest it made me feel absolutely phenomenal. I was on an adrenalin rush for weeks. It got to the point where I would go out of my way and add time onto my journey to drive down the mega-posh mansion road for a good old beep and scream.

There might be someone reading this book who lived down that road and remembers the mad screaming bloke. The best part was when I would wake someone up and they would shout at me from their double-glazed sash bedroom windows to 'shut the fuck up'. Then I would shout back, 'I'll shut up when you open up the road, you helmet!' I always find it fun to call someone a helmet. It's such a soft but degrading put-down.

I have always enjoyed a good scream. It's the easiest way to release energy, especially when you have no outlet. I thought I was the only one who would scream into a pillow for a release so I could relax or get to sleep. But then I read Frank Skinner's book, where he talks about screaming to unleash his pent-up frustration. I was so happy to know I wasn't the only one. Plus he is one of my comedy heroes, which if anything endorsed the screaming and pushed me to do it more. So if there's another young wannabe comic reading this, have a good old scream – it will make you feel better. But you will have to write jokes and do thousands of gigs. Screaming isn't enough on its own.

I used to go out drinking in central London with mates when I was younger. Without the car it would be an hour on the night bus home. A taxi home was completely out of the question, far too expensive. I used the night bus a lot during my early days of comedy and boozing. I was young, naive and oblivious, but the night bus system in London is terrifying. It's like the film *The Purge*, all sorts of creatures come out to play.

The thought of my daughters getting the night bus home from central London gives me heart palpitations. Just typing this now is starting off a minor panic attack. I don't want to be an overbearing and overprotective parent, but I also don't want to be a parent who chucks their kid in shark-infested waters. I can see myself driving into central London to pick them up from a nightclub. Trying to get gigs at comedy clubs near where they go out and pretending it's a strange coincidence so I can drive them and their mates home.

Growing up, there was a character-building mentality associated with the night bus – 'it's good for you, it makes you experienced, streetwise and appreciate things'. Which I agree with in parts, if you want to become 'the best at night buses', an arbitrary title that must be hard to officially crown. You will need to travel on a night bus a lot if that's your goal. I don't think you need to have used night buses in order to appreciate things. You can live your life without going on a night bus and you will be absolutely fine. The same way I have never been beaten up in the street. I don't need to be beaten up in the street to appreciate not being beaten up in the street. I understand that it's an awful thing to happen and I will try my best to avoid it.

Let's be honest: nobody on a night bus wants to be on a night bus. People are either drunk or working night shifts, sitting there thinking, *Why did I get so pissed?* or, *Why didn't I learn to drive?* I once saw a man on a night bus have a shit in a bag, tie it up and pop it in his pocket. He wasn't embarrassed or ashamed. In his defence he was on the back row of the top deck of the bus, which somehow seems classier and more socially acceptable. He wasn't drunk or on drugs, just a man who really needed a shit. But the efficiency and speed with which he managed to squeeze one out and then organise it neatly into his pocket implied that it was a regular part of his average day. It's something you don't think is possible until you see it happen. I would like to add that watching such an event once is enough for life.

On one particularly bleak week, when I was about 22, I got the night bus home from work three nights in a row. This was when I worked in an office, so I wasn't working a night shift. I went to the pub after work at 5 and stayed there all evening, missing the last train home from Charing Cross. It's not an early last train, either. It was at 00.53 a.m. For those three nights I kept the exact same schedule. At around 2-ish I would buy a McDonald's Quarter Pounder with Cheese meal then eat it on the bus and fall asleep, hopefully waking up near my stop. I did this Wednesday, Thursday and Friday night. I would go to work all day then repeat. I would survive the mornings with a Greggs bacon turnover and a Lucozade. One really depressing flashback I get is of holding a Greggs bag in the queue for a McDonald's breakfast. That image just screams fat-boy pisshead. Then, as the hangover was starting to kick in, I would go to the pub at lunch for a pint, which would solve that problem, then muddle through the afternoon until the pub again at 5 p.m.

I can't believe I didn't get sacked. I actually fell asleep in a meeting once. My boss shouted my name to wake me up and I said, 'Whoops! I had a little sleep there, didn't I?' But somehow I remained employed. I was starting to get really good at falling asleep, a skill that has gone up to the next level since having kids. Put me in a chair in a quiet room and I am gone in under ten minutes. Cinemas are the worst – they're so dark and cosy. I slept through the entirety of *Avengers: End Game*. Sure, Thanos might be loud, scary and aggressive, but he's not as loud, scary and aggressive as the New Cross one-way system where I was sleep-trained.

It's weird how easily and deeply I can sleep considering how energetic I am. I am all or nothing and I get powered up by other people's energy and enthusiasm. I can go for days and days if you keep putting me in front of people or a crowd. But if you then put me in a room on my own, I'm out like a light. Lou finds it so irritating, as I never hear the kids when they cry at night. She is always woken up first and lies there waiting for me to wake up because it's my turn to deal with them, but I never do. Don't worry, when Lou is away and I'm home alone with the kids I wake up to help them – it just takes a bit longer.

The deep sleeping might be a class thing too, as my house was so compact and chaotic and everyone worked weird shifts. My dad would come home late from cabbing, my brothers worked in bars and restaurants, I would be up at 4 a.m. on a Sunday to work at the flower market. The routine was all over the place – especially when you shared a bedroom. I would be in bed asleep at 11 p.m. and my brother would come in from work and fire up the Dreamcast for a game of *Crazy Taxi* or *Shenmue*. I could sleep through anything. In Lou's house growing up, she had her own bedroom and her dad worked a solid, regular nine-to-five office job. It was a much calmer and quieter family home, whereas my house was full of people 24/7, like a home for drifters. You would go downstairs on a Sunday morning and five of my brother's mates would be sleeping on the floor. I loved that mad, busy house growing up. You would meet so many characters. Once, when I was about 14, my mum said, 'Can you find somewhere to sleep this weekend because your auntie is coming to stay and we need your room?' So I went to my mate Oli's house and got an unbroken eight hours' kip on his bedroom floor.

People would just knock at your door and come in for a tea or a coffee unannounced. It was only when I met Lou that I learned middle-class people don't just turn up. You have to wait to be invited, which I have always found very unambitious. Middle-class people need to have a bit more faith in their banter, plus not care about how messy their house is. My mate Steve was dropping me home from playing golf one day and needed the toilet, so I invited him in. The house was bit untidy, as Lou had been indoors with the kids all day. But Lou lost her mind and apologised to Steve as if he had just walked into a murder scene, pleading with him not to tell anyone about what he saw. Steve didn't care at all. People actually like visiting a messy house, as it makes them feel better about their own house when it gets messy. It's like a morale-boosting public service.

My parents didn't give a shit growing up. There could be 50 kilos of heroin, an AK-47 on the kitchen floor and Shergar in the garden and my mum would still invite my mates in for a sandwich. That's not because we were dirty, it's just that we didn't care what people thought of us. Our house was always clean but it was very messy. Mainly because there were on average at least five people living in a three-bed terraced house with one toilet. It was impossible to keep it showroom tidy; by the time you finished tidying it up someone else would make it messy again. My mum tried to enforce an official closing time of the kitchen at one point to stop us undoing all the cleaning and tidying she had done. The house was always busy. You couldn't keep on top of it. It was like trying to clean a moving car – any progress you make will be pointless. But a middle-class person's house has to be clean and tidy before you can visit at the pre-agreed time. The middle-class dream is for the house to look like no one lives there.

When I lived in Lewisham it looked like nobody lived there because I spent most of my time drunk on night buses. I'm a born and bred deep sleeper, the night bus is where I did my sleep A levels. On one occasion I missed my stop and woke up in Eltham, about a 15-minute bus ride away from my house. It was 4 a.m., I was groggy and drunk, so I jumped off the bus and crossed the road to wait for another bus going back towards my house. I sat there in the freezing cold for 45 minutes, only to be presented with the exact same bus with the exact same driver. The driver was absolutely pissing himself laughing as he said, 'Welcome back on board, silly bollocks.' That was night three of my night bus hat-trick, and I thought to myself, *This has got to stop.*

JOBS

I have had so many jobs. I've worked on the markets, in shops, in pubs, flyering, as an office temp, cricket steward, waiter, admin assistant – the list goes on. A number of classic dead-end jobs, all in order to pay for booze, holidays and bills. One of my first jobs was stacking shelves at Sainsbury's when I was 16. I was paid £3.61 an hour and I was livid. I couldn't believe how crap that was, but it was money. I also had the worst shifts in the history of part-time jobs. I would be at sixth-form college during the week studying tourism, and I would work Fridays and Saturdays, 2–10 p.m., on the cheese, milk and yoghurt aisle. An absolute two-pronged social-life killer. First prong was that you missed out on going out on Friday and Saturday nights. Prong two was that if you did manage to get to the pub before closing you stank of cheese, milk and yoghurt. But I put up with the bad shifts because I wanted money and I wanted to feel like a grown-up.

I loved that job. It's so much fun as a 16-year-old to meet new people and hang around with proper adults. There is also something liberating about having a job you don't really need. Sure, it was nice to earn my own money, but I had no bills or responsibilities. I could walk out whenever I wanted and that's a feeling that doesn't last long. Real life catches up with you quick. Before you know it you've got a mortgage and a family so you need to stack those yoghurts like a good boy or your life will come crashing down. I would swagger around those aisles like an outlaw, an untouchable maverick Sainsbury's cowboy. All I would think was that if they sacked me I would just apply for a job at Asda. I didn't have a care in the world.

Having a uniform was like getting to wear fancy dress, but for a real reason. It's not fancy dress for the sake of it. I'm a fan of dressing up but I'm not a fan of fancy-dress parties. I've always found that they are thrown by people not confident in their personality or ability to have an interesting conversation unless they are dressed up as Crocodile Dundee or MC Hammer. I think I am still scarred by being talked into wearing fancy dress by an ex-girlfriend for her friend's birthday.

I really didn't want to wear fancy dress but it was early in the relationship, so you make compromises/do whatever they tell you. It was a house party with a beach-club theme. My then girlfriend and her friend, the birthday girl, were wearing normal clothes but with a hula skirt pulled over their jeans, a flower garland and sunglasses. I was wearing flip flops, board shorts, a vest and a life jacket. I've got no idea why I was wearing the life jacket. I probably thought it would look funny because you know me, I'm a bit of a laugh. Okay, the truth is that I wore the life jacket because I wasn't confident enough to wear just a vest.

Anyway, I was a bit nervous, as the only person I knew at this party was my then girlfriend. We got there first to help set up and then about 40 people arrived over the next hour. Absolutely no one was wearing fancy dress. They were all wearing normal clothes, as there was talk of going to a nightclub later that evening. My then girlfriend and her mate started to feel a bit self-conscious in their beach-club outfits so they removed the hula skirt, garland and sunglasses and were left in normal clothes. I, however, did not have that luxury, so I spent the entire house party in flip flops, board shorts a vest and life jacket. Can you imagine introducing yourself to people for the first time dressed like that? Ever since then I have been wary of fully committing to fancy dress.

I still remember how powerful the Sainsbury's uniform made me feel. On my first ever shift I was pushing a pallet of Müller Corners around a corner, which always used to make me laugh. As I was doing this a mum was shopping and her toddler was in my way, so she said, 'Come over to Mummy and let the man through.' Let THE MAN through. That's right, I am a man and you are letting me through. Not only am I a man, I am 'the' man. Up until that point I had always been a boy. But now I was a man. I couldn't believe it. This promotion had come out of nowhere. I barely had any pubic hair, and the ones I did have were blond so you couldn't really see them. When I first started sprouting my man hairs they were so fair that I once actually coloured them in with a black Sharpie so they would be more visible. But forget my bald dick and balls for a moment, if you can. I know it's hard but please try. I was officially a man and it had been confirmed by a grown woman in the cheese aisle of a supermarket. I think it was the cheese aisle.

I was a late developer when it came to puberty. I have vivid memories of wanting pubic hair more than anything in the world, to the point where I would inspect my arm-pits with a magnifying glass to try to find any sign of life. I would spend hours looking, like NASA trying to find life on Mars. Eventually I did fully pube up to the maximum, and what an anti-climax it was. Being hairy is horrible. It smells, it needs trimming and it spreads. I've got a hairy back. No one wants a hairy back. It's the worst type of body hair and you need help to trim it. You can't deal with it on your own. You just have to pathetically ask your wife, knowing that she hates doing it but it's the only way it will get done. In the summer Lou makes me stand in the corner of the garden, facing the fence like a naughty dog. In the winter I stand in the shower and she shaves me like a pet chimpanzee.

I loved working at Sainsbury's, but that's because I was a terrible employee. I enjoyed 'working' there because I did no work. My approach to that job was, *If I am getting paid £3.61 an hour, no matter what happens my chal-*

lenge is to do as little work as possible in that time. How unproductive can I be and still get paid? I saw the eight-hour shift as a personal challenge. What could I get away with this week? I used to walk up and down the aisles for hours, looking for a product that an imaginary customer wanted. In reality I was just chatting to my mates who worked in different departments.

I always used to try to work on Sundays, when the clocks were going back or forward. I would arrive at work an hour late and pretend that I'd got confused with the clocks going back or forward. Whatever the clocks were doing I would go in late. I don't know how I didn't get sacked. I was destined to be self-employed, as I could not understand why I would work any harder than the absolute bare minimum if I wasn't earning more money for the effort.

This attitude carried on in the office temp jobs that I did. I used to make people cups of tea all day long. I had a technique to make it take ages. I used to fill the kettle up to the maximum limit with the coldest water I could find. I would run the tap on cold for ages and if there was any available in the freezer of the office kitchen I would put ice in the kettle. Lumps of actual ice in a kettle to slow the boiling process. This made sure it took about 18 minutes for the kettle to boil. How much did I hate my job if I would rather stand in the kitchen trying to boil ice?

I know what you are thinking: if I loved making tea so much why didn't I get a job in the hospitality sector? The answer is that I did get a job in the hospitality sector, as a waiter in the ill-fated restaurant chain Caffé Uno. I lasted about five shifts. I was a terrible waiter. I hated being a waiter because on my first shift it dawned on me that I don't care what strangers want for their dinner. I don't really care what I want for dinner. I don't even care what my wife and kids want for dinner most nights. So spending an evening asking strangers what they wanted bored me to tears. I couldn't give a shit what these randoms wanted, which was quite problematic, as I had to tell the kitchen to make it. Plus, I couldn't wander off for hours to help imaginary customers. So my advice to a 16-year-old reading this who wants a part-time job is to get yourself to the biggest supermarket you can find and get a job stacking shelves. Make sure you stay quiet during your induction so not too many people notice you. Then when you start work just walk around with purpose at a high speed and you can avoid doing any actual work for hours at a time.

Before I started doing comedy it was obvious that I was not enjoying my job. But there were no alarm bells. Everyone I knew hated their job. My dad did not enjoy driving his taxi for 12 hours a day but it paid decent money that he could use to provide for his family. One of the most exhausting things about being working class and trying to be or do something different is the fear of failure. The thought of coming back home with your tail between your legs, admitting defeat. The fear of not being able to provide.

When I finally left my day job to become a comedian I had just broken up with a girlfriend I had been with for a couple of years. This was it, the big leap into the unknown. The safety net of the day job had gone. I had done it, I was a comedian. I would be introduced as 'Rob the comedian', not 'Rob who works in an office and does a bit of comedy on the side'. I was a fully signed-up member of the clown club. It was a completely fresh start. I had left behind an old career and an expired relationship. The relationship actually ended because she thought I wasn't ambitious enough. Anyway, back to my book I am writing all on my own.

My new career as a comedian had begun; however, the main problem was that no one was actually paying me to do comedy. It's very hard to claim to be a professional if you earn no money in your profession. My income was very up and down was the diplomatic description; the truth was that I was earning about £250 a month. So, in order to help pay the bills, I would do a bit of flyering outside Tube stations. On one occasion I handed a flyer to my ex-girlfriend, who was coming out of the station en route to her well-paid job in the City. It was mortifying. We didn't end on bad terms but it's always awkward seeing an ex at the best of times. When she asked the innocent but completely loaded question, 'How's the comedy career going?' I went instantly red. I then proceeded to lie and make up a number of gigs and TV shows I was working on. It was all complete and utter bollocks. What made it worse was that I wasn't even flyering for a comedy show. It was just a normal flyering job for some shitty overseas mobile phone minutes, texts and data plan.

I found trying to be something different terrifying. I remember when I first started doing comedy shows, I kept it as a secret from my family. I was still living at home with my parents and two of my brothers, sharing a bedroom with my younger brother Joe. I hadn't told anyone I was doing comedy to avoid any 'banter', which is basically horrific verbal abuse that really goes up a level when you are related by blood. As brothers we were pretty brutal to each other. Our nicknames for each other were so horrible. My eldest brother had acne all over his back so he was called 'dartboard back'; Joe had bad breath once for about three hours but was known for years as 'dog-shit breath'. I had large puffy nipples brought on by a hormone imbalance during puberty and my nickname was 'Jaffa Cake nips'. Even my parents had nicknames: you already know that my mum was Big Suze, which was because every penny you borrowed off her went into a little black book like a debt collector. My poor dad had slight man boobs so he was called 'jugs'. My mum used to call it the house of no compassion. So, I think you can understand why I felt I couldn't come out as a 'comedian'.

* * *

I never thought about or was ever asked what my passions were and where I wanted to be in life. Get the money in was the always the plan. There was no time to ponder what I actually wanted to be. It was all about providing and keeping afloat. When you're trying to survive there's no time to think about how you could thrive. That's how I thought everyone lived their life, and it's only as my life has moved on and I've arrived in different circles that I've realised how wrong I was.

I recently worked on a TV quiz show with Emilia Fox, a brilliant actor who stars in *Silent Witness*. I had never met her before but she was absolutely lovely and great on the show. Whenever you have a guest on a TV show the researchers always produce a bio on the guest detailing their life and career and any information that might be of interest. As I read her bio, I couldn't believe how completely different her background was to mine, but somehow we had got the same job, were working together and, on top of that, we got on so well, like old friends who must have loads in common. For those who don't know, Emilia is from an acting dynasty. Her parents, her brother, her uncle, her cousins, her grandparents were actors and one was a theatrical agent. She went to a private school and learned to play the cello, piano and trumpet. She can speak French and German, and she finished her education at Oxford University.

Now, on paper, my working-class chip on my shoulder absolutely hates the idea of Emilia Fox and everything she stands for. The reality, though, is that Emilia is one of the nicest, most unassuming people I have met in the industry. She couldn't have been more chilled, polite and humble. What really struck a chord with me was her ambitions growing up. In a press interview she was asked about coming from a family of actors and whether she wanted to follow in their footsteps. She answered, 'Quite the opposite! I don't know if it was just being a rebellious teen, opposed to everything my parents stood for, but I made a conscious decision at an early age that I would not be an actor. So, I went to Oxford Uni to study English literature and my aim was to be an art critic.'

First of all, I love that in the world Emilia comes from, going to Oxford and studying English literature to be an art critic is an act of rebellion. Normally a teenage rebellion involves the local park with drugs and alcohol. Not Emilia. She's up at the National Portrait Gallery with a notebook, the fucking rebel. I think it's amazing that her aim was to be an art critic. What a wonderful example of having the confidence to dream of being whatever you want to be and going for it. I still cannot believe that being an art critic could ever be someone's job, never mind an ambition as a kid. Sure, there's lots of art and it needs to be critiqued. But no one aims to be an art critic, do they? Surely you just fall into it. You can't say out loud that you want to be an art critic, can you? Could you imagine the scenes in a careers lesson at a South East London comprehensive school if you put your hand up and said you wanted to be an art critic? You would get abused for years for that kind of behaviour.

I at 23 still couldn't tell my family I wanted to be a comedian. But I don't really know why, as my family have always been so supportive. Sure, there would have been some piss taking, but deep down they would have wanted me to succeed at whatever I chose to do. It was just that it was such an alien concept I couldn't even imagine that conversation. There would never be an appropriate moment to bring it up. When they did find out they were so supportive and always have been. Maybe it was more my own issues than any pressure from my upbringing. Either way, I didn't want anyone to know.

I had read an interview where Eddie Izzard said that you can't call yourself a comedian until you had done a hundred gigs. I was on gig number two so I was officially still just a Jaffa-nipped twat having a go. I was so concerned about my family finding out about my gigs that I used to walk laps around my local recreation ground while saying my jokes out loud to remember them. To this day I still don't write any material down. I just say it out loud at a gig and if they laugh I remember it and say it again next time.

In moments of self-indulgence and artistic pretence I tell myself that I don't write down any of my material as comedy is a spoken art form, and if I write it down on a page to remember it I create another barrier between me and the audience. The funniest comedy needs to be as direct as possible from thought to laugh. In reality I imagine it's much more sensible to write it down but I was too afraid of my brothers finding it and taking the piss out of me for it.

So walking round the park was my best option. I didn't have my own bedroom to practise in and the house was too small. You couldn't have a shit in that house without everyone being aware of what you were doing, let alone bang out a comedy routine in the hallway mirror. We are potentially moving house soon to a place where my daughters would each have their own room with an en-suite bathroom. That blows my mind. Lou said to me, 'They would only be small en suites, though, Rob. Probably only big enough for a small bath.' I was like, 'Are you winding me up on purpose? "Only big enough for a small bath". Oh, how will our poor girls cope with just a small bath each?'

I am trapped in a constant battle between wanting my daughters to have nice things so they have a lovely life, but also wanting them to struggle sometimes so they can appreciate working hard. But I think the two extremes are wrong. I want to try to pitch their experiences somewhere between 'dog-shit breath' and 'their own en suite'.

In the end the truth came out about my gigging because everyone knows everyone in South East London. My mum found out about my first ever gig about an hour after I had done it, from two separate sources. My mum's mate's son was at the gig by chance and reported back to his mum. Then, on top of that, my mum's friend Debbie had rung my mum earlier in the day to share some concerns about my behaviour. Debbie's house overlooked the recreation ground and she had watched me walk laps of the park while talking out loud to myself for three hours. You can't get away with anything when your mum is Sue Beckett, Social Queen of South East London.

Mum now dominates the social scene of Murcia. My mum and dad have an apartment in Murcia, in southern Spain, on a new development aimed at Brits. The weather is always beautiful and there is a really strong community spirit between all the Brits who own and rent apartments out there. They are all pals and all know each other and look out for each other. Which sounds lovely but when I visit it's a nightmare. You can't relax, as everyone wants to talk to you. However, it has nothing to do with me being on the telly. In Spain I'm one of 'Sue's boys', which means you become a minor celebrity. I'm talking winner of *Big Brother 4* kind of level. All her friends want to talk to us about our life and kids because they have heard so much about us from my mum.

My mum knows literally everyone in the south of Spain: British ex-pats and the locals. When her neighbour Pedro comes round for a barbecue the conversation is all done on Google Translate. My mum can't speak Spanish and Pedro can't speak English, but boy do they love a barbecue and chatting through iPads. I find it astonishing, the information she has on people. You will be sitting round the pool and she will say, 'He's the air-con man, remarried for the third time last week', 'He sorts out the broadband but he's only got one leg', 'That bloke does an Elvis tribute act and airport runs for cash in hand'. I should point out that the Elvis tribute and airport trips are separate businesses. He doesn't dress up as Elvis to drive you to Alicante. But I'm sure if you chuck him a few extra euros he will. I once saw a Neil Diamond tribute act in Spain that refused to do 'Sweet Caroline'. Imagine being a tribute act with artistic integrity.

My parents love us boys and the grandkids more than anything and they would do anything for us. I reckon I could get my dad to kill someone if I told him someone was nasty to me or my kids, which is a really big power move that I don't really want to be implementing any time soon. But it's nice to know I have it in the locker. All my parents do in Spain is lie in the sun getting browner and drunker, and talking to their neighbours about their boys. My dad's back is so brown that when he sits on a wicker chair topless he looks like a Louis Vuitton bag.

Because of the Beckett Boys Spanish PR machine, me and my brothers can't get a moment's peace when we go out to Spain to visit. You will settle down next to the pool then a random deeply tanned northern ex-pat will come up to you to ask which one of Sue's boys you are. 'Are you the tall one?'

What kind of question is that? Surely he can make a judgement on my height. I'm only 5-foot-8. If I'm the 'tall one' the Becketts must be half-Borrower. 'No, that's Joe. He's the tall one. I'm Rob, nice to meet you.' You will then be subjected to them repeating everything Big Suze has told them about you. I was once reminded by a Geordie that the MOT and tax were due to run out on my Nissan Micra. I forgot about renewing it once and my car got clamped, and ever since then it's been my parents' sole mission in life to remind me about my MOT and tax at every given opportunity to stop it ever happening again. So random conversations with leather-faced ex-pats can be quite informative if you've forgotten to update the DVLA with your new address.

It's a strange experience when your 12-year-old Nissan Micra gets clamped. You sort of re-evaluate your original purchase decision. I thought to myself, *I don't think it's worth paying to get it unclamped. I might just leave it here for ever to rot. Why did I buy a Nissan Micra in the first place?* I've upgraded since to the Japanese King of Dad cars, a Nissan Qashqai with a roof box, and I hate that car just as much.

Please don't get me wrong, my parents' friends in Spain are lovely people. Jeanette and Tony are a really kind couple who are great value on a night out. I always try to catch up with them when I gig up in Liverpool. They are also really good friends to my parents out in Spain. However, sometimes when I'm out there sunbathing on 'holiday', I don't need a stranger to give me a full run-down on why Wigan Athletic are currently struggling in

League One and why they got relegated in the first place, just because they shared a jug of sangria with my mum nine months ago.

I'm not overegging this, either – it really happens. My parents know hundreds of people who holiday out in Spain, which means they have a network of associates all over the UK. My parents could run a county lines drug cartel with their phone book. I was once out on the piss after a gig in York, and when I was drunkenly walking back to the hotel at 2 a.m. I heard 'Jardin 5' shouted at me outside York Minster.

'You what?' I said in a drunk and confused state.

'Jardin 5. Sue and Dave. You're one of Sue's boys, aren't you?'

My mum and dad stay on Jardin 5 when they're in Spain so it clicked. I gave him a thumbs up and a 'Yes, mate' and stumbled home.

My parents' popularity has actually helped me as a comedian. It's like having a free two-person marketing department. If only my parents were from Oxfordshire and called Jemima and Barnaby, they could have sold out my whole Edinburgh Fringe run. Luckily for me they have more power and influence in the UK-wide live touring scene. I did a show in Newcastle and my mum and dad came and stayed with their friends from Spain who lived nearby. After the show my mum said, 'Can my friends come backstage to say hello?' I said, 'Of course.' Within five minutes there were 28 Geordies in my dressing room asking me which one of Sue's boys I was. 'I'm the short one who does comedy. You just watched me for an hour and a half.'

We all went to a pub after and it was so intense trying to find a seating area for 30 people. I had walked off stage straight into a combined Geordie stag and hen do. To be fair most of my parents' pals had bought tickets, which was very kind of them and I'm very grateful for their support.

Free tickets and the guestlist are always a nightmare when you're from a working-class background, as we love a freebie. When I played Croydon on my last tour my brother Darren asked for some tickets to the show. Which of course is absolutely fine. I love my friends and family coming along to support. Actually that isn't strictly true – I love it when certain friends and family come to my shows.

The main problem with friends and family at a show is that they know you too well and get too comfortable. The Becketts are not great at observing social rules at the best of times. Put ten of them in a row at one of my shows and it's like they can't see the hundreds and sometimes thousands of other people in the venue – as if it's just a private performance for the Becketts. They also know some of the stories I tell, especially as I talk about my family and upbringing a lot on stage. In some cases a family member in the audience might be the star/victim of a particular routine. Which is problematic, as they will instantly know if I have bent the truth slightly for a better punchline. After the show they will take great pleasure in pulling me up on certain aspects of the story, cross-examining me on the accuracy of certain details such as dates and locations like I'm in the Old Bailey on a murder charge, and completely missing the point that it was just a joke and I tweaked the information slightly for a bigger reaction. I am already predicting that I will have to gather witness statements from my mum and brothers to prove that we called each other dartboard back, dog-shit breath and Jaffa Cake nips.

In general, though, I genuinely do enjoy having my friends and family along to watch me at work. Barring the odd heckle from a pissed-up brother, naming no names. Russ, it's always Russ. He either heckles or talks quite loudly throughout the show. I sometimes give away meet-and-greet tickets for charity raffles – free tickets to the show, and I meet the winners for a photo and a quick chat in the interval. These tickets are normally in the guest-list block of seats reserved for friends and family. At one tour show the charity raffle winners asked me if my brother was in the audience. They had heard him talking during the show, probably giving a live commentary on the veracity of one of my routines. I imagine it went something like, 'Nah, it weren't the Berlin stag do he shit himself on, it was the one in Malaga. I remember it. We had dodgy paella. I told him those prawns were on the turn. That's why I had cheese omelette and chips. I'm calling bullshit on that one, bruvva.'

In Russ's defence he didn't wait for me to be famous to start heckling. Sure, he has heckled me at the Hammersmith Apollo in recent years, but he also heckled me during a show early in my career at a Stockwell pub back in 2011. You've got to give him respect: he has been there with me from the bottom to the top, shouting out at me along the way.

At the Stockwell pub show I had a representative from a DVD company in to watch me, as they were interested in signing me on a development deal. DVDs were mega back in 2011 and companies would sign new acts on deals so that in five years' time, when they were ready, they would release a DVD with them. Unluckily for my generation of comedians the word 'streaming' was invented and the arse fell out of the DVD market. But early 2k 10s, I think that's what we are calling it, having a DVD company rep talent scouting at your show was a huge deal, as you could secure a hefty paid advance to help with the bills as you learned your trade as a comic. So the pressure was really on to deliver.

It was an intimate venue, with only 25 to 30 people in the audience, including Russ, who halfway through my show walked past the stage and said, 'Rob, I'm going for a piss. Do you want a pint?' This happened in the middle of my show. He didn't shout, like a traditional heckle, as the room was so small. On top of that the laughs were so quiet that night it was possible for him to politely ask me if I wanted a drink and the entire audience would hear. I of course said yes and he wandered off for a piss and a pint.

I don't think his behaviour was acceptable but I can understand that it must be hard to see anything other than your brother on a stage. No matter what your siblings are or become, you still think of them as that annoying eight-year-old in your house. For example, I still think I could take my younger brother Joe in a fight. The truth is that I would have no chance. He's 6-foot-4 and about 17 stone. But in my head he's my little brother that I could knock out with a clean one-two.

Anyway back to my other brother Darren and his request for tickets (side point: he had heckled me at the Croydon show on a previous tour). As much as I love doing my job, it's still work and the aim is to make a profit, otherwise I can't pay the bills and Lou gets cross. My tour is my production but the admin is run and operated by a promoter that books the venues and organises all the logistics, marketing and ticketing for an agreed percentage split. With free tickets for your family and friends, there is normally an unspoken rule that it's two or four tickets per person who puts a request in, as every free ticket given away is a cost for the production. This system works, as I want all my friends and family to come, but there needs to be a cap on numbers. When Darren asked for some tickets to the Croydon show I said, 'Yep, no worries, Darren. How many tickets do you want?'

His response was, 'How many can you get?'

How many can you get? Like I'm nicking them from a warehouse. I said to him, 'The answer to that is all of them, Darren. I can get you all 2,000 tickets if you want. But if I gave you all of them I would be operating at a loss.'

In my experience the 'how many can you get?' mind-set is a class thing, as normally a working-class person is employed by a company, maybe in a shop, an office, a factory or building site. So we are back to the victimless crime of fiddling and quid pro quo. Now, as a self-employed touring comedian I have essentially become the company. A company that consists of the boss of the company and the sole employee going on stage in front of thousands of strangers to talk about shitting himself in either Berlin or Malaga, depending on your sources. So even though it doesn't look like it, I am running a business.

After big shows like the Hammersmith Apollo in London there is a bar that all of the people on your guest list can go to afterwards. I can see all my friends and family there. This bar is normally a free bar, as it's paid for by the production. In this instance, though, my show is the production, so I will have to pick up the bar bill. Which is all good, as I have sold a decent number of tickets and it's nice to buy everyone a few drinks to say thanks for their support over the years. But some of my friends and family are completely oblivious to that. They will say, ''Ere, Rob, come and have a drink, it's a free bar. We're all on triple Jack Daniel's and cokes. What do you want before the free bar runs out?' All I am thinking is, *This is not a free bar. For me it's the most expensive bar I've ever been to in my life. I've bought about 400 drinks. I've got four gas fitters smashing back six triple whisky and cokes an hour like it's their last night on earth.* To be fair, this show took place at the Hammersmith Apollo on 7 March 2020, about a week before Lockdown 1, so it basically was the last night on earth.

Now, I don't want to sound like I'm moaning or that I'm stingy. I was happy to pay the bar bill, but I find it interesting that, in my opinion, due to the class background of my friends and family, there was no awareness that I was footing the bill. The strange thing is that if my friends and family knew I was paying the bill they would most probably insist on paying for their own drinks and even offer to buy me one. But in their minds there is a faceless comedy company in the sky that will pay the bar bill, so all they are thinking is, *Let's make the most of it.*

When Lou and I were thinking of names for our first child, I asked my mum why she had picked Daniel, Robert and Joseph. Her response, I think, sums up an ambitious working-class mentality. She said they were names you could use in an office or on a building site. Oooh, go on, Big Suze, with a plan of us working in offices and not driving a taxi or van. It was aspirational and I love it. However, she didn't want to go all in at the employment poker table with Dorian, Rupert and Jasper. Daniel, Robert and Joseph can easily morph into Danny, Bobby and Joey. I can imagine Danny, Bobby and Joey arriving to finish off the tiling in the kids' en-suite bathrooms. 'Don't worry, lads, it won't take long – the en suites are only big enough for a small bath.' I don't know about you, but if my boiler was broken I'm not sure I would trust someone called Tarquin to fix it. The same way I wouldn't hire a barrister called Gary.

For some reason working-class people like to play down their jobs and their skill sets. From downplaying how impressive what they do is to downplaying their actual job titles. Being a gas fitter, for example. What a strange thing to call yourself. It's such a geezer job title: I get gas and fit it in your fucking house. Do you want gas in your house, because if you do I can fit it in? You know the middle classes would describe themselves as heating-installation engineers. One of my mates started a new job, and when I asked him what he did he replied, 'I put in all the pipes in pubs.' No job title there, just direct and no messing. I do 'pipes in pubs'. Now that has got to win geezer job of the year.

My mum's naming plan worked perfectly when I got my first job at the age of 14 at Coutts bank as an intern. Of course I didn't – it was at Columbia Road Flower Market. My job was to stand outside a shop, selling bags of compost to all the East London hipsters who didn't have a car to drive to Homebase.

Weirdly, to this day me and my brothers are all crap at DIY. I am definitely the worst by far. Joe and Dan are getting better at it. I think that stems from seeing my dad always lose his shit when he tried to do DIY. I never managed to learn from him, as he was either too angry to communicate or I was still laughing too much from his previous outburst to concentrate on his advice.

Once, he had to varnish the garden furniture. A classic dad job, it's got to be up there with going to the dump and taking everything out of the shed and putting it back in again for no apparent reason. As a dad now, I have realised that the reason they do the shed re-arranging is just to get away from their family for a few hours. Especially if it's nice weather. It looks like you're doing something but the reality is that you're just sitting near your shed having a beer in silence, pretending to be productive.

Anyway, back to the varnish. As he was carrying the tin through the house, he tripped over my mum's wooden Birkenstocks on the floor. Firstly, he screamed, 'Fucking shoes!', picked them up and threw them into the garden. So that immediately sent me completely hysterical with laughter, and when I go, I go. I sound and look like a bald chimp in distress. Then, when he saw the spilt varnish on the carpet, he delivered some of the greatest swearing I have ever heard. To this day it's still the best. He looked at the floor and said, 'Oh, you bollockie cunt.'

I heard this and I went into overdrive. I couldn't breathe. I still don't know what that means and I'm still not sure how you spell it. Is it bollockie with the 'ie' or bollocky just with the humble 'y'? I was slowly dying from oxygen deprivation when he turned to me and finished me off with the final line: 'If you keep laughing at me I'll fucking varnish you in a minute.'

I was bright red and my head was about to explode – I had never laughed so much. Then my mum walked in and said, 'Even if you tried to varnish him you would probably spill it.' She'd done him like a kipper. She carried on: 'Now go and get my Birkenstocks. I'll phone the insurance and put a claim in. While you're spilling stuff why don't you pour some on the stairs – I've been wanting new carpets upstairs.'

I thought that, as my career in comedy and television progressed, I would get further and further away from working alongside working-class people and the kind of people I grew up with. Which in part has been true, but it also weirdly comes full circle. In the summer of 2020, I got a small acting job in a new Hollywood movie, a remake of the *Cinderella* story to be released in 2021. Now, without sounding like Billy Big Bollocks the Bad Boy Brigadier of Bragging, this was a huge deal for me. I was shitting my pants. One, because it was a big Hollywood film, but also because it was a Disney film and my daughters are obsessed with Disney princesses.

The triumph of making it into a Disney film was slightly marred by the bittersweet part. I played a pervert. Thomas Cecil is an older, slightly lecherous man who wants to marry Cinderella, which is a great part to play, as it is all comedy and I could mess around and be funny. The downside is that my children will see me with a ponytail and a beard perving on Cinderella. Not ideal, is it, as you drop your kids off at the school gates. Is your dad the sex pest from that *Cinderella* film? Yes he is.

All stand-up comedians can act to a certain degree. You are playing out scenes in your routines onstage every night, so you learn that skill. However, you don't learn all the little extra bits and bobs that you would learn at acting school, so whenever I'm on an acting job I'm very much learning as I go. I was obviously very nervous about the job. I had a few pages of script to learn and on top of that my character had a limp. With my limited acting experience I had no idea how to act like you have a limp. Sure, I can limp, but how do you keep it consistent?

When I went to the costume fitting, I told the costume guy about the limp. (Job titles are the sort of things you learn at acting school – I don't think costume guy is correct.) He told me there was an old acting trick where you just put a stone in your shoe and that way you will limp and it's the same every time. I could have kissed this geezer. What a legend. I finished the fitting and I was skipping with joy all the way home. *I know how to limp, I've learned my lines and I'm bursting with confidence.*

The next day, I arrived on set. I was given a ponytail wig and make-up, and then got into my costume. My character is a retired military man so my costume was a formal military style, all tough, heavy and rigid material that took two people to put me in. While they were dressing me, I held onto my trusty limping stone. I popped it into my boot, they strapped the boots up and I was ready. The costume involved my trousers being physically attached to my boots. No idea why but who was I to question it? Stone in and boot on, I started limping onto set to start my life as Hollywood's go-to pervert. I would like to state for the record that I am more than happy to be typecast as a pervert if it means a long career in film.

My nerves started to build as there were about a hundred people onset and cameras everywhere. It was a much bigger set-up than any TV I had ever done. Plus, my scene was with Cinderella and her stepmother, played by Camila Cabello, the American-Cuban music superstar, and Idina Menzel respectively. For those who don't know, Idina Menzel is a Broadway megastar and also Elsa from *Frozen*. Fucking *Frozen*. A film that basically babysat my daughters for three years. They were both so lovely and put me at ease straight away.

I started to relax. I knew the lines, the other actors were nice, I had my limp. *Let's do this*. The director grabbed me to run my lines and it all went well. Then I asked her about the limp and how pronounced it needed to be. She said, 'Oh, no, your character hasn't got a limp. He's lying and using a walking stick for attention and sympathy. So we need to get shots of you walking normally to prove the limp is a lie.'

I replied, 'Yeah, cool, of course. No problem.' On the surface I looked calm and composed. Inside I was exploding. *You fucking what? No limp? But I've got a fucking stone in my shoe which has given me an actual real-life limp!* I had given myself a limp for a character who didn't have a limp, so now I needed to act like I didn't have a limp even though I had an actual limp. I only gave myself a limp because I didn't know how to act like I had a limp.

I know what you're thinking: *Just take the stone out of your shoe, Rob.* I wished I could but I physically couldn't, as it took two people to get me dressed, my boots were strapped to my trousers and I couldn't even reach my feet because the uniform was too rigid and I wasn't flexible enough after putting on a stone in Lockdown 1. On top of that, someone had given me a basket of fruit and veg to carry as part of the scene and the director had just shouted, 'Action!'

I kicked the floor with the front of my boot to try to dislodge the stone. No luck. I trudged forward with a look on my face that was trying to say, *I'm a retired military perv who wants to woo Cinderella.* In reality my face was saying, *This stone is fucking killing me.* With filming, everything takes hours, so I slowly got used to the pain, but what calmed me down more was the atmosphere on set.

It was a Hollywood movie but we were filming the scene near Slough, with a mainly British crew. Obviously movies are full of actors and creatives, but there are also hundreds of other jobs necessary for a film to happen: lighting, set building, rigging, props, stunts – the list goes on. A lot of these jobs are done by working-class geezers. I was an outlier when we were shooting the scene opposite superstars like Camila Cabello and Idina Menzel and being directed by the amazing Kay Cannon. But when we stopped filming to set up the scenes, I felt like I was back at the market. All these massive blokes with big, thick hands came out of the background to move stuff or build something. I was chatting to them all and it was like being back in South East London. The stunt woman was from Bexleyheath – just down the road from me, where my mum used to go to bingo.

It gave me a weird sense of calm to know it wasn't an alien world where I was going to get found out as an imposter. Everyone on the set was extremely talented and deserved to be there doing their job. Sure, your background can help you get to those jobs quicker or slower because of your opportunities and privilege. But the main thing that will stop you is your own self-belief. If you tell yourself that you can't do something you will never be able to get there.

The truth of it is that the anticipation of a job or an occasion is always worse than the reality. Before I did a Hollywood film, I could have predicted a million different scenarios where it would go wrong or people would be mean to me and I wouldn't fit in. I would never have thought a geezer called Terry would laugh and say, 'I bet you're regretting that fucking stone now,' and offer to help take my boot off while I had a chat with a girl from Bexleyheath about Gala Bingo and when Cineworld did £2 tickets on a Tuesday.

HOLIDAYS

I absolutely love a holiday and I have probably been on every single level of holiday, from Slovakian hostels to ski resorts, from Butlin's to Center Parcs, and from Benidorm to a private island in the Caribbean. Some of these trips have been with my family, friends and Lou's family, and some for television shows (see skiing and the private island). But what is a working-class holiday? The price will have an impact, as usually the working classes have less disposable income than the middle and upper classes. However, it's not always about the money; sometimes it's about the things you do when you are away on holiday. I think I have been on the most stereotypically male working-class holiday that has ever existed.

In the summer of 2012 I performed at the Edinburgh Fringe for the whole of August, sharing a flat with my good friends and comedians Kishore Nayar, Lloyd Griffith and Romesh Ranganathan. After an exhausting month of flyering and the daily pressure of performing an hour-long solo show at the world's biggest arts festival, me and Lloyd decided we wanted a little holiday to relax and recuperate.

Kish had to go back to his day job as head of legal and Romesh had to go back home to his family – the pair of losers. Me and Lloyd were kid and head-of-legal free so we booked a three-night stay in Majorca. Lloyd is from a working-class background in Grimsby and, along with me, can sometimes find the class divide at Edinburgh and in the comedy industry tough to navigate. Before I tell you what we did on this holiday I want you to know that none of it was planned. It just naturally happened and only now, looking back, it was obvious that we both subconsciously found the Fringe hard to experience. We gravitated back to the comfort of our working-class roots on a holiday that made us feel normal again.

We arrived on the Monday and sat by the pool, then in the evening we went to an English bar because it had free Wi-Fi. We had some food that came with chips then drank four pitchers of lager while watching *Monday Night Football* on the telly. We didn't support either team playing but it didn't matter. After the game we went next door to a nightclub and watched a tribute act, which was the Jackson 4, who did the Jackson 5 back catalogue. But none of them looked like the Jacksons. They were all different races and one of them mimed. After the tribute act, we went into the arcade and competed against each other on the punching machine like a couple of legends. Can I get an 'Oi, oi, saveloy'?

On the Tuesday we sat around the pool in the evening, went to the same English bar to use the Wi-Fi then ate something with chips and drank four pitchers of lager while watching the Champions League football. Again, we support neither team. After the game we went next door to watch the tribute act, which was the self-titled One Tonof Fun, a larger-than-life female performer who did soul hits. She had a great voice, to be fair. I'd argue more than a ton of fun. After One Ton had finished singing we went to the arcade again to compete against each other on the punching machine. I should add that during the cabaret shows we drank cocktails and were stag-do level pissed both nights. Lloyd beats me at punching hard again. We go to bed.

The final night of our holiday. Pool all day, back to the English bar in the evening. Wi-Fi followed by something with chips, followed by pitchers of beer, all while we watch another Champions League football match featuring two teams which, again, we don't support. After the match, off to the tribute-act night. Robbie Williams is in town – called Robbie Willy Arms, or something like that. We watch Robbie tear it up then go to the punching machine. This time I beat Lloyd because I get a high score and, as he puts his final 50 cents into the machine to punch, I run up and punch the machine on his final go. He has no money left for another opportunity to beat my punch. I am victorious on a technicality. This makes him absolutely furious, to the point that we actually start having a drunken fight. One Ton of Fun is in a nearby bar on her night off and breaks up the fight. Me and Lloyd have a final drink for the road and make up. We stumble home, go to sleep, wake up the next day and fly home from our 'holiday'.

I was 26 on that holiday and I look back on it now, as a 35-year-old father, and think to myself what a fucking brilliant holiday that was. I have zero regrets. I had a quality time. However, stealing Lloyd's last go on the punching machine was a bit out of order and I would like to take this opportunity to offer Lloyd a written apology and extend the invitation for a rematch. Covid-dependent, I think it would be great for that rematch to take place at the book launch. In all seriousness, I loved that holiday. We could have, if we had wanted to, afforded a slightly more expensive resort or a more remote location with fewer tourists, but we didn't want that. We needed that recharge of normality after the alien environment of the Edinburgh Fringe, which for us was beer in an English bar in Spain, watching football we didn't care about.

A holiday is a massive indicator of class; it was one of the ways I realised Lou and her family were posher than me. They invited me on a family holiday to Center Parcs. But not any old Center Parcs trip, a Center Parcs trip in the school summer holidays. Yeah, man, big money shit. Sure, most people have been to Center Parcs in February when it's freezing cold and about £40 a person. But Center Parcs in August has a different breed of clientele paying the premium. Saudi princes and sheikhs flying down the rapids. Elon Musk and Warren Buffet duking it out on the badminton court, using rolled-up £50 notes as shut-tlecocks.

It felt strange for me to be at Center Parcs, like I was behind enemy lines. I was Butlin's through and through. You could cut me and I would bleed red. I don't think that turn of phrase works with something that's red, as your blood is already red. But you know what I mean. I had convinced myself that I wouldn't like Center Parcs, but I loved it and I felt guilty. My favourite thing about it is that you can sit in the sports bar in a tracksuit and not be judged. You can't do that on any other middle-class holi-day than Center Parcs. Yes, I am having a pint of Stella in an Adidas two-piece, but I've just smashed a nine-year-old at indoor short tennis so it's allowed. I've got bowling at 2 p.m. followed by archery at 4. I don't have time to slip on some jeans and shoes for this drink.

I remember my father-in-law talking to me about how the clientele was changing at Center Parcs and it wasn't as middle class as it used to be. I was thinking to myself, *I know, mate. The reason it's going downhill is me sitting opposite you, drinking a pint.* It's so silly but I think that when you grow up not being able to afford a certain thing, you tell yourself that it is overpriced, not worth the money and you wouldn't enjoy it anyway. It's not for people like us. But the truth is, you're only thinking that because you're trying to protect yourself. It's a lot easier to feel like you're not missing out if you convince yourself you don't want or like something, rather than really wanting to go somewhere that's unobtainable because of money or connections.

When I had less disposable income, I would always get steak from Morrisons or Asda and say, 'That's lovely steak at a good price – why would you want to get it from anywhere else?' I wouldn't have dreamed of buying Marks & Spencer steak when, for the same money, you could eat out at the Harvester on the early bird special. Steak from Morrisons and Asda is decent and I eat it, but recently I have been eating steak from M&S, which is more expensive but it is much nicer. But a few years ago, when I couldn't afford M&S steak, I would tell you that it tasted the same as Morrisons and Asda steak. I was just lying to myself in order to not feel like I was missing out.

I can't explain why I feel this weird guilt and shame for admitting I buy steak from M&S. I get an overwhelming sense that I'm being wasteful or flash, or that I've changed and forgotten where I've come from. It's such a weird thing to be embarrassed about. Is it a British thing or am I just being mental and overthinking it? In America you would be celebrated and praised if you had worked yourself to a position to be able to afford expensive steak. You would put it on Instagram and everyone would like it and be positive in the comments. I would be really embarrassed to post my weekly food bill from M&S on social media. Maybe no one really cares and all this is internal and I'm beating myself up for no reason, but when I'm in the M&S

food hall a self-critical voice pops into my head and starts giving me grief: 'Look at this flash prick in M&S. Too good for Morrisons now, are you?' Other people aren't giving me stick – it's just my inner monologue. One thing I will say about Marks & Sparks is that calling their shop a food hall stinks of pretentiousness. It's a supermarket with aisles. Get over yourselves, Mark and Spencer.

Now, apply that same mentality to holidays. It's the same thought process but on such a bigger scale. Before Lockdown 1, in February 2020, me, Lou and the girls went to Barbados for ten nights, stayed in a lovely hotel and flew premium economy. It was a big celebration holiday after I'd finished the first leg of my tour, which had sold out. Even now I am trying to justify my holiday to you, the reader. I don't need to. It's my life and I can do what I want. But the voice in my head compels me to justify it and/or apologise for it.

On the way back BA offered us the chance to upgrade to business class for a pretty good price. I thought we were just lucky, but looking back it seems obvious that BA realised Covid was going to stop air travel so they were trying to get as much money in as possible. So we decided to upgrade, which meant that my two children, at the ages of two and four, were going to be flying in business class. They each had their own seat that magically transformed into a full bed, big enough for a full-grown adult. I'm not going to lie to you, it was absolutely glorious. Both children lay in their beds in silence with their iPads for an hour, then they both slept for six hours. It was one of the greatest flights of my life. In fact, it was one of the greatest nights of my life, full stop. Me and Lou sat up chatting and drinking wine in peace.

I didn't tell anyone that we flew back business. It was our little family secret. I can't really explain why but I was embarrassed by it. We got home and the next day I was getting the four-year-old dressed for nursery. She was excited to tell everyone at nursery about going to the beach for a holiday. I refused to tell her it was Barbados, as I was not psychologically ready for my child to say the word Barbados out loud.

I'm aware that this plan had no longevity, as she would get older, start to read, understand more things and I wouldn't be able to pretend every holiday we went on was to 'Spain'. But at that moment she was four years old and illiterate. As far as she was concerned she went to 'the beach' for a holiday, and I was happy with that. This was the perfect crime. I could have the holiday I wanted without people knowing, so I could silence the critical voice in my head. I then asked my daughter what her favourite part of the holiday was. She replied, 'My favourite part of the holiday, Daddy, was on the plane when my chair turned into a bed.'

I was almost physically sick. The plan had burst into flames. Everyone at nursery would know we had travelled in business class. Or even worse, they might assume it was first class. As silly as it sounds, I actually had a slight panic attack. I've had a number of these moments with my children. They normally occur in front of my parents.

My mum and dad have moved to a two-bedroom house in Margate, on the south-east coast of England, to retire. It has a pretty compact garden but still big enough for a six-person table, shed, umbrella, barbecue and a section of grass. This makes the garden sound massive but all of the things I have just listed are touching each other. When you are working class you do not let the lack of space stop you from having things. I live in a four-bedroom home in the South East London suburbs. We have a decent-sized garden but nothing out of the ordinary for the suburbs, though it's about five times bigger than the garden I had as a child.

When me and my children arrived at my parents', my mum said, 'Girls, do you want to play in the garden?'

They squealed, 'Yes,' in excitement and my mum led them outside. We were all in the garden and my three-year-old turned to my mum and said, 'Nanny, where is the garden?'

Again, almost physically sick. Oh my God. I went instantly red and wanted to curl up and die. What do you do in that situation? You can't tell your child off, as they are too young to understand what they have said and they haven't actually done anything wrong. Also, if you do tell them off it implies that the garden is obviously small and they were being rude by highlighting it. What my mum decided on was walking them to the local park and telling them the park was in fact their garden. So now my kids think Nanny and Grandad's garden is six acres and includes swings, a climbing frame, skate ramp, tea hut, three football pitches, and teenagers drinking cider and getting off with each other in the corner.

I don't know why my daughter's comment made me feel so awkward. It wasn't in front of a stranger – it was my parents' house. My parents didn't care; they thought it was funny. In a way, it's a compliment about the way they brought up me and my brothers. All of us have bought our own homes and have had successful careers. In a way, if your grandchildren have a happy and comfortable upbringing, totally alien to yours, then you have done a great job. The hard work and opportunities my parents offered us enabled us to have a different lifestyle to them. As a family you want generational growth and progress. I hope that one day my grandchildren will look at my garden and think, *Poor old bastard. He had to live with this shitty tiny garden all his life.*

That trip to Barbados wasn't the first time I had travelled in business class. I had done it in the past for work. I think because someone else was paying and it was a work trip it didn't bring the same kind of shame. The first time I travelled in business class was on Emirates to Australia to film *I'm a Celebrity ... Get Me Out of Here! Now!* I felt like I had won the lottery or one of those Andi Peters competitions on *Good Morning Britain*. It was like being in a dream or in virtual reality. I couldn't believe I was

Bromley boy on tour. One of my first comedy appearances at a music festival, in a pair of boat shoes and skinny jeans.

I've got no idea why I'm on the floor, nor why I'm wearing a bin bag as a coat. But I do know it was the first time I'd sold out the Hammersmith Apollo and achieved my dream.

This photo was taken while filming with Romesh in South Africa, where I hit my lowest point and wanted to give up on everything. Just goes to show that you should never judge a book by its cover. I'm so glad I got through that period as I became a little too good at being able to hide how I was feeling.

I can hear panto calling my name louder and louder these days.

Don't want to brag, but this is me in an actual Disney movie, albeit playing a pervert. Still, how many Disney films have you been in as a pervert or otherwise?

On *The Jonathan Ross Show* in 2019. Wossy was a hero of mine growing up, and it's an honour and a privilege every time I get to be a guest.

Me on *I'm A Celebrity . . . Get Me Out of Here! Now!*, the spin-off show to *I'm A Celebrity . . . Get Me Out of Here!* Do these captions count towards the word count?

It's always great to meet my fans post-show. Back L–R: John Bishop, Lenny Henry, Judi Love, Jimmy Carr and Russell Howard; front L–R: Romesh Ranganathan, Rosie Jones, Kerry Godliman, Alan Carr and me. Taken at Wembley Arena after a charity do.

Me and Phil Kerr – he's one of the funniest people in the world, one of the best comedy writers in the business and one of my best mates.

My manager Danny Julian me, Romesh and his manager Flo Howard, four working-class people celebrating us hosting the Royal Variety Performance at the London Palladium. It almost felt like an *Ocean's Eleven* working-class heist.

Me and Romesh in Times Square recreating our most famous scene in *Rob & Romesh vs*. I pretend I've got a career as a stand-up comedian, but a lot of my work is just taking my clothes off for cash.

This is a photo of some bald bloke at a charity show getting to meet comedy megastars Rob and Romesh.

On the floor again, this time better dressed.

Hosting the Royal Variety Performance with Romesh is one of my proudest moments. I love this man.

Still hosting the Royal Variety Performance, but not as proudly this time.

there, and my working-class mindset kicked in. I had to make the most of it because I might not get to do it again. If this was my one and only chance I had to make sure I experienced every single moment. I had a duty to do everything you could in business class and report back. I ate everything that was offered, pressed every button that was on the seat. I logged into the Wi-Fi and sent an email for no other reason than because I could. I was so eager I actually emailed myself the words 'I've sent this on a plane' before we even took off, which undermined the whole thing.

I went to the bar and had a bowl of olives and a Martini. I hate Martinis but if you are on an aeroplane that has an actual bar in the middle of it you can't have a can of lager and a packet of scampi fries. Even though I would have fucking loved some scampi fries. So I sat at the bar, grimacing and hating every single sip of my drink, thinking I looked like James Bond. Whereas in fact I looked like a competition winner dressed in Emirates pyjamas and Emirates flight socks that no one else actually puts on. They also give you a little leather toiletries bag with aftershave, moisturiser, toothpaste and all sorts of goodies.

When we landed and were leaving the aircraft, I did something I regret. I've never told anyone, but if you can't be honest in a book where can you be honest? As I left the plane I noticed that some lunatics hadn't taken their free leather toiletries bags. They hadn't even opened them. I call them lunatics but I think the proper term is frequent flyers. People who fly business so much that they don't want the bag of freebies. Animals! Anyway, I noticed all these unopened leather bags of freebies and I took them all. As I walked down the plane I grabbed eight of them and stuffed them in my backpack. I think I technically looted a plane. When I got home I wrapped them all up and gave them to my family as Christmas presents. Why? Because they were free. I had found a little fiddle, a victimless crime that would benefit me and my family. The exact same mindset that my friends and family had with the free bar at my tour show.

The problem with business-class travel is that you instantly get used to it. I'm talking immediately. It almost ruins travelling, as you now know what luxuries are beyond the curtain. Before I travelled business I could tell myself it was a waste of money and not worth it. Ignorance was bliss. After I came home from Australia in business, I went on a trip to Iceland with Lou and some friends. We flew on a budget airline in economy, which took about five hours from London to Reykjavik. Halfway through the flight I was bored and thought to myself, *I'll go to the bar for a drink*. I started walking down the aisle and slowly realised that there was no bar on this plane. It took one flight in business to change me. That's the problem with experiencing nicer things – you want them more. That's why I'm a huge fan of the ignorance is bliss approach. It's hugely underrated and underappreciated. Sometimes it's simply better not to know there is a better option.

However, ignorance is bliss doesn't always work. I have been a victim of this approach. We booked the Iceland trip for December, in the middle of the Icelandic winter, when it's minus 10 with four hours of sunshine per day. That holiday wasn't bliss; it was dark and fucking freezing. But it was a cheap deal and I love a cheap deal. Well, I used to love a cheap deal until my trip to Dubai in June 2015. I was so excited about the cheapness of this deal. The flights were cheaper than flights to Spain. I remember shouting out loud, 'I can't believe the flights to Dubai are cheaper than the flights to Spain!'

We got such a cheap deal mainly because it was the middle of the summer in Dubai. Dubai is in the desert and, as we know, deserts are well hot. Now, this wasn't just hot – it was hot for Dubai hot. On the day we arrived it was 45 degrees outside. Degrees Celsius, not Fahrenheit. FORTY-FIVE. I've slow-cooked pork on 45. It was so hot that when you left an airconditioned building to go outside your glasses steamed up, like when you open the oven door to check on your roast potatoes. It was actually too hot to wear a polo shirt. I've never known so much heat. Imagine it being too hot for a polo shirt. I was sitting outside in a polo shirt thinking, *I'm gonna have to cut the collar off in a minute to try and cool down.*

We tried a camping holiday once as a family when I was about eight years old. Only because me and my brothers wanted to do it. My parents are very much Spanish sun and cocktail people. We did the most inner-city working-class approach to camping. We drove for 20 minutes out of London to the first bit of green we could find and camped for two nights in a tiny field. Our camping holiday was located in zone 6 of the London transport system – technically it was reachable on the Tube. My mum does not like dirt or animals, and on the morning of the second day of our holiday she drove home to our house for a shower.

I don't think working-class people like camping deep down. The point of camping is to get back to nature and be close to your family without all of life's luxuries. But when you grow up in a small house sharing a bedroom with your brother, the last thing you want to do is sleep even closer to him. Plus, the cost of camping might be cheap, but the initial outlay on all the gear is extortionate. I went camping in the summer of 2020, when Covid stopped most travel. I had zero equipment and I basically spent about a grand in Decathlon, which is basically a cross between Aldi and Sports Direct. Brands you sort of half-recognise but the spelling and wording is a bit whacky. We bought so much stuff it was like *Supermarket Sweep*, two trolleys piled up. I kept saying to myself that we would be spending more on flights and hotels if we were going abroad. Which was total bollocks. In order to get my money's worth I would have to force my family to go camping every year for 15 years. On top of that I had to buy a roof box for my car because I couldn't fit all the camping stuff in my boot.

We went camping for three nights in gale-force winds and I got about three hours' sleep in total. I spent the rest of the day sitting on a fold-out chair drinking coffee in an exhausted daze. It didn't feel like a holiday; it felt like my house had been demolished by a tornado and I was at a temporary emergency rescue centre working out the next steps to rebuild my life. But on the plus side the girls loved it. It was such a novelty for them and the little sickos didn't seem to be at all disturbed by gale-force winds ripping through canvas at 3 a.m.

One thing I never realised people owned was walking shoes. We never had walking shoes as kids but apparently that's a thing. A pair of shoes solely for walking. What are you doing in all your other shoes, levitating? But then I started walking in lockdown and realised that if you go for long walks and you don't have walking shoes, you get blisters and back pain. Growing up, I just thought everyone got back pain and blisters after walking loads. I didn't know there were shoes for it!

As a kid you had three pairs of shoes: school shoes, your old trainers and trainers for best. For weddings you might get a new pair of shoes that were a bit big and by September they'd turn into your new school shoes. But walking shoes, just shoes for walking, seemed excessive. I now own a pair of walking shoes and I can't imagine a world of wearing my trainers for a two-hour walk. What was I thinking, bowling around a nature trail in a pair of ice-white uncreased Air Force 1s like a nutter?

Gore-Tex has been a revelation for me. You can go anywhere with a pair of Gore-Tex booties on. There is no puddle or mud that can get in your way. I felt like Iron Man the first time I put on a pair of Gore-Tex walking boots. Nothing could stop me. I had confidence in my all-terrain, all-weather footwear. Maybe I have become fully middle class? The conversion is complete now that I own Gore-Tex walking shoes. But maybe not, as middle-class people don't seem to be as excited about how effective Gore-Tex is at keeping your feet dry. When my enthusiasm dwindles for my dry trotters then I imagine I will become a full member of the middle-class walkers society. I'm sure there's a round-robin newsletter I can join or a forum where they complain about planning permissions.

I just never really realised that there was official equipment for activities. Back in the day I would just wear what I owned for whatever it was I was doing. When I was about 25, I did shows at the Altitude Comedy Festival in Austria. It's a combination of skiing in the day and comedy gigs in the evening. I got paid for the gigs and free ski hire and a ski pass. I went skiing on my own, in Austria, in a pair of skinny black jeans from River Island. I would say one of my best personality traits is also one of my worst at times. I am super-positive with a real 'it will work itself out' energy, which is great because it means I'm productive and I can get stuff done. However, it does also mean I will end up on the top of a mountain freezing to death in a pair of skinny black jeans from River Island. I also had no idea how to ski, so I basically fell over at the top and dragged myself down the slope on my back like a dog wiping its arse on the floor. While being laughed at by posh English seven-year-olds who could ski perfectly. Is there anything more annoying than a child who can ski? I can't work out if it's because they have been taught to ski from a young age or they are such annoying little shits that the only way their parents can cope is to throw them down a mountain to get a bit of peace and quiet.

The best holiday we had as a family was repeated every year for about ten years, and it brings back some of the most treasured memories I have as a kid. We used to hire a villa in a place called Jávea, on the Costa Blanca in Spain. It had four bedrooms and a garden and private pool. We used to get it at a reduced rate from my dad's friend. I never asked why we got it cheap and my dad never told me, so I think it's best if we leave that question unanswered.

It was the absolute best. We would sit by the pool all day then go down to the seafront in the evening and have dinner. We had the old, trusty *menú del día*, a set menu where you got a starter, main, dessert and drink for a bargain price. My mum and dad still have them every day when they visit Spain. When I was a kid it was pre-euro and you could get a three-course meal for about 250 pesetas, which worked out about £4 each. I don't think we ever ate off the à la carte menu in the ten years we visited Jávea. It was strictly *menú del día* and a Fanta Limón every night.

We were in our own villa and we felt like film stars. It was an unbelievable feeling. The best part of it was that we were only a 45-minute drive from Benidorm, so we could still visit for the day but go back to the villa in the evening and feel superior. We'd try to tell ourselves that we weren't Benidorm people any more, even though every time we went there for the day my parents would insist on going to an English pub to eat fish and chips and have a cup of tea. Surely they could survive two weeks without battered cod and chips, you'd think, but there was absolutely fucking no chance of that. There are some things that just don't change. Fish Friday is Fish Friday. You can't have a Spanish omelette on a Friday. So my parents would drive us to Benidorm to sit and eat fish and chips in 35-degree heat.

I've always struggled to eat fish and chips in the heat. It's a cold-weather dish. I tried eating it and I was so hot my knees started to sweat. I had sweaty knees. Not even just on the back of the knee – on the front too. I didn't know it was possible for the front of the knees to sweat. You can't eat something deep-fried and battered in the Spanish sun when the fronts of your knees are sweating. You need an ice cream and a lie down.

One of the most stressful things about an overseas holiday with my mum and dad was the rental car and petrol. My dad is obsessed with the price of petrol and diesel.

How it normally works when you hire a car is that you take the car with a full tank of petrol, which you pay for in advance, then you return the car empty, as if you leave petrol in the tank you won't get a refund. This for my dad was a challenge – a challenge to beat them at their own game. No one is going to get one over on Dave Beckett. If you want this petrol tank on empty then I'll give you this tank on empty – and oh, boy, he did.

I can remember him driving for an hour from Jávea to Alicante with the petrol light on and the dial beyond the empty marker. It was so far off the empty marker it was actually closer to full as it approached a full revolution of the dial. I have no idea how we made it to the airport. The car was running on fumes, willpower and my dad's refusal to be beaten. We were pleading with him to put more petrol in the car. But he refused, like an old Spartan warrior taking on a whole army alone, with no shield and a broken sword. At one point I'm sure I heard him mutter to himself, 'I'd rather miss the flight than put another drop of petrol in this motor.'

But he was right. We made it without breaking down. He had worked out the petrol miles per gallon and he knew best. There are things in this world that my dad doesn't know much about, but when it comes to cars and petrol Dave Beckett is like a fucking professor with a PhD in geezer.

I can sit here now and tell you that I have absolutely zero idea what my car does, miles per gallon. Me and Lou went to Spain for a holiday a few years ago and I gave the rental car back with half a tank of petrol. This sudden rush of panic and shame came over me, like I had done something wrong. I was thinking, *If my dad knew about this he would be so disappointed in me*. What a weird thing to worry about. So I sat down and tried to work through it. I did the maths and it basically cost me about £20 to give it back half-full. I didn't need that petrol – I had made it to my destination. What was the other option? Get to the airport three hours early and do laps of the car park to get my money's worth?

I think when my dad reads this he will answer yes to that question. But I will have to disagree with you there, Daddio. Let's put it this way, reader: would you rather give them half a tank of petrol and be £20 down or give them an empty tank and be evens but have the horrible anxiety that you are going to run out of petrol on a Spanish motorway and miss your flight? I know my answer. Take my £20 immediately so I can relax. I'm happy to be mugged off by the rental company if it means I'm not about to hyperventilate on the AP-7 toll road.

My dad and fossil fuels have a long and intense past. I don't know why but whenever we drive past a petrol station he will comment on the price and compare it with other local garages and their prices. Maybe it's because he was a professional driver for over 50 years or it's that he used to deliver petrol and diesel to petrol stations all over the country. I couldn't tell you why, but I do know one thing. Do not get him started on the price of petrol at motorway service stations. The thought of having to fill up at Clacket Lane services on the M25 would make his face turn red with rage.

The best part about Spanish holidays in the 1990s was the evening market where they sold fake clothes and bags. I was an addict, and my crack was fake football shirts with player names on the back. We couldn't afford the official versions back home, especially not the extra £15 for a name and number. I bought five shirts one year for the price of one real one. The kits were decent-quality fakes but some of the other stuff was dreadful. Anyone for a pair of Roy Bins sunglasses? How about a Lewis Vuitton leather bag? The worst was a leather 'Nike' belt. Nike didn't even sell leather belts – can you counterfeit something that doesn't exist?

As much as I loved these holidays to Spain there were a couple of bad experiences. On one trip, when I was about 13, I lost my gold RB ring. This was a birthday present from Argos, an alleged gold ring in the shape of my initials. At the time I was devastated that I had lost the ring, but in hindsight it might have been the greatest thing that ever happened to me. It's not a good look, is it? The RB gold ring, especially for a 13-year-old boy with a matching gold chain. At the time I loved it. When I was growing up everyone wore gold – it was the fashion. My Dad had a gold chain, gold watch and gold rings. I wanted to be my dad when I was little, and wearing gold was the first step.

I was too young for the matching swallow tattoos on my forearms. That would have to wait until my fourteenth birthday.

I still have a soft spot for gold sovereign rings and I plan to treat myself one day, if Lou will let me. At the moment she is absolutely 100 per cent dead against it. Super Dave no longer has any gold because he sold it all for cash during the 2008 recession, which is how gold ownership works in the working classes. Buy it high and sell it cheap. Buy it back high again. It makes the most sense.

The gold and the outfits of teenagers in 1990s South East London were something to behold. Girls would wear gold chains with gold clown pendants out on display on top of their Bon-Bleu jumpers. Boys would wear Von Dutch caps with the peak of the cap pointing to the sky so they could still put wet-look gel on their fringe. Weirdly both sexes would wear trackie bottoms tucked into their socks. Normally a Kappa tracksuit tucked into Winnie-the-Pooh socks.

People talk about the nineties as being a great time for fashion. I disagree. It looked like everyone worked the bumper cars for a travelling fair. Even infants were involved in this look. Six-month-old babies would be taken to Claire's Accessories in the Glades shopping centre in Bromley to have their tiny little ears pierced with a gun. The most minuscule little full-stop dot of gold in their previously perfect little ears. I know you shouldn't judge, but if you have had a baby's ears pierced I just want to say

I judge you and so does everyone else. We may not say it but we are all thinking it.

As well as losing my beloved RB ring, the other bad experience on holiday in Jávea involved my nipples. As you know, by the time I was 13 I had already been christened 'Jaffa Cake Nips' because of my large nipples, but on this holiday my Jaffa nips pushed whole new boundaries. As puberty kicked into overdrive they got even bigger, plus I was putting on weight. It was the perfect nipple-enlargement storm. On top of puberty and my weight gain, the Spanish summer made my nipples swell in the heat.

My nipples on that holiday were fucking massive. I am talking double-take-in-the-street massive. Like you've just seen Elton John on a penny-farthing with a boner juggling dildos attention-grabbing massive. They were like a pair of Wombles' noses sniffing about the Costa Blanca of their own volition. Like when you kill an octopus but the tentacles still move about on their own. I was so insecure about them that I hardly took my top off for the whole holiday. The worst part was that they were so prominent you could see them through my T-shirt. I was so self-conscious, I used to constantly pull at the middle of my T-shirt to try to get the material off my giant nips, which actually made it worse. There would be a strange bump in the middle of my top where I had been pulling at the material, which made people notice my chest more because it now looked like I had three giant nipples, with one slightly smaller and sharper in the middle. It was a great look for old Bobby Massive Virgin Beckles.

I get frustrated when people talk about the teenage years being the best of your life. Yeah, for the good-looking athletic ones with normal nipples I'm sure it's great. But for me I found it an awful experience. I was fat, I had no confidence and the tits of Dolly Parton. So if there are any teenagers reading this who are having a tough time, I just want to say that you're going to have to ride this one out. Don't beat yourself up if your teenage years are crap. That's fine. They are for most people. Just know that it will get better and all the little things you are worrying about now, you won't give a shit about once you are older.

I hated my body so much, to the point that I looked into getting surgery for my nipples. There's some sort of condition that gives you large nipples and the solution is having some fat and breast tissue removed. I didn't have to do that, as my nipples reduced in size when I lost my puppy fat and finished puberty. Don't get me wrong, though. I've still got a fairly chunky set of nips on me. But, as I was informed by my GP, they aren't medically large any more. At the time I thought I would never be topless in front of anyone – friends or partners. I was genuinely worried that I would never meet anyone and be able to have an intimate relationship because I was so worried and ashamed of my body. It's mad how your feelings about yourself can change. As I have got older and become more confident, I don't care any more. Obviously my body isn't perfect and I would like to lose a bit of weight and get fitter. But there is no embarrassment or shame any more.

My body has actually become a comedy asset in my career. I've been topless on TV in front of millions of people a number of times. I hosted the *Royal Variety Performance* in front of Prince William and Kate Middleton in an ill-fitting Lycra catsuit. I did a modelling shoot with Romesh in tiny Speedos and the TV company projected the image on a hundred-foot-high advertising board in the middle of Times Square in New York. I find it funny now, but if you had told me at 13 that was going to happen I would have thought you were on drugs. It's much easier to laugh at someone who looks like me rather than David Beckham. But let's be honest, if I could look like David Beckham and I wasn't allowed to do comedy, I think I would still take that swap.

Can you imagine the holidays David Beckham has been on? Not only would they be somewhere beautiful and luxurious, but he also gets to literally have the body of David Beckham on the beach. I don't think I'll ever be truly comfortable with going on nicer holidays. I will always feel like a competition winner to a certain degree. But I hope to accept that and be able to enjoy it. It's such a waste of time analysing and overthinking when the point of a holiday is to relax. Plus, I've worked hard to enjoy a nice holiday and I should be able to enjoy it like anyone else. If I am brutally honest, whenever I am on holiday I will always look at my kids and think to myself, *You lucky bastards*. But I won't say it out loud and make them feel guilty or like they have done something wrong. I will just think it in my head, which I think is maybe not ideal, but it is progress.

FOOD AND DRINK

If you asked me the name of the best restaurant in the world when I was 15, I would know the answer straight away. New Ming Chinese all-you-can-eat buffet in Welling. The all-you-can-eat buffet is the pinnacle of dining when you are from a large working-class family. All you can eat is not an offer, it's a fucking challenge. Not only was it all you can eat, it was ordered off a menu and brought to the table. No queuing for a sweaty, shiny buffet. We are talking about the crème de la crème gold standard of all you can eat. I'm talking duck on tap, mate. You could eat five crispy ducks if you wanted.

We went there for every birthday and special occasion for about ten years. In that time I don't think we ordered anything other than tap water to drink. Why? That's where they make their money, on the drinks. New Ming wasn't really a dining experience – it was a food to pound-note hustle. It was like beating a Vegas casino. The joy wasn't in the taste of the food – it was in the victory of getting your money's worth. People would ask how our dinner was and there would be no mention of flavour or ambience.

The response would be, 'We had mussels, prawns, crab, duck and lamb and it was only £11 each.'

To be fair, New Ming was tasty, but was it the best in the world? Not for most people, but in the small world of a young Bobby Beckles, New Ming was the GOAT. All I can remember is pure joy in that restaurant, and I've eaten in some lovely places in my time. But nothing has matched that excitement and buzz of being in New Ming. What made it more exciting to a family with teenage boys was that the name of the restaurant was so close to being New Minge. We would wind up my mum with threats to order New Minge special fried rice to cause her maximum embarrassment. We would always bottle it once the waiter was there, as most teenage boys are all talk and no action. However, in what was one of my greatest memories of childhood, my mum slipped up one time and accidently ordered 'New Minge special fried rice'. We all absolutely lost it with laughter, including the waiter. My mum had just 'minged' off the waiter. It was a historic moment in the Beckett family.

It wasn't all fun and games, though. Once, much to the amusement of me and Dan, Joe got reprimanded for his overzealous and aggressive use of the lazy Susan. The wooden turntable that allows all diners to access the food was being clawed at and spun around by Joe so he could grab the last chicken satay, while people were still serving themselves. He spun it at such speed the food went every-where. Even when the food is unlimited sibling rivalry will rear its competitive head. It didn't matter that you could order more – Joe wanted *that* satay. If my memory serves me correctly, he was taken outside of the restaurant for a talking to and a cool down. I can guarantee you that I'll get a call off my brother once he reads this, calling 'bullshit', but it's how I remember it.

My parents have always been quite adventurous eaters, which rubbed off on me and my brothers. On holidays in Spain, alongside the classic British fish and chips in Benidorm, we would travel to fishing villages like Calpe to have fresh seafood and paella. My mum would always say, 'Try it, it might be your favourite,' about absolutely everything. Which didn't really hold up when her teenage sons would respond with the offer of human shit. How about this, Mum? Try it, it might be your favourite? Another one of my mum's classic sayings would come out after we had all sat down to eat dinner. Once it was served and we began to eat, every single time she would say, 'Ooh, must be nice because nobody's talking.' But if we were to talk she would say, 'Stop talking with your mouth full.' For her it was a win-win – nobody would speak through fear or enjoyment.

We were not the stereotypical working-class family who would call a pasta bake 'weird foreign food'. However, in our extended family we did have that element. I think it's more a generational issue than a class issue. I think some people get to 65 and just refuse to experience anything else. They have decided, *I'm 65, I don't have time to waste trying something new. I need to spend these last few years enjoying what I already know I like.*

I had an uncle who refused to eat rice. I mean, who doesn't like rice? It's one of the most inoffensive foods available. It's like not liking bread. I was sitting with family members once, watching a television travel show in China where they were eating Asian street food. One of the dishes was a scorpion on a stick, and I remember an uncle saying, 'Look at the fucking state of that. It's absolute filth. A scorpion on a stick? These people are weirdos,' as he ate a bowl of jellied eels. Completely missing how ridiculous he looked.

Now, as a resident of South East London, where pie, mash and eels is the king of food, I need to make a public statement: jellied eels are the worst food ever made. They're like a cockney bushtucker trial. I love pie. I love mash. I love beautiful green liquor with loads of salt, pepper and chilli vinegar. I even love stewed eels. I love my local delicacy. But jellied eels can fuck right off back into the sea, the Thames, the sewer or wherever they catch the slimy little shits. They are the work of the devil. It's like someone woke up one morning and thought, *What shall I do today? I think I will try to ruin jelly for everyone.*

How are you going to do that, Gary? Everyone loves jelly. It's a kids' party classic.

I'll tell you how I'm going to ruin jelly, Jason. I'm going to take away the strawberry flavour, make the jelly look like thick lube, keep the eel on the bone and ram it straight in a bowl of translucent jelly.

I don't know if you have ever seen someone eat a jellied eel. It will haunt your dreams. A portion of eels will be four or five bits of eel, each one exactly the same size as a person's mouth. The victim/diner will pop it in their gob and have to use a combination of teeth, tongue and sheer willpower to manipulate the meat off the bone. Once it's mission accomplished, after 30 to 40 minutes of tongue acrobatics, they will spit eel bone into a tissue next to their plate. Jellied eels have to stop. There are some traditions that need to die out. People talk about how great tradition is, but some can fuck off.

My kids don't like pie mash. To be fair, they tried it when they were really little and since then we have been in lockdown and the pie-mash industry hasn't sorted out the drive-thru system yet. At the moment most pie-mash shops shut at about 2 p.m., so a 24-hour, lockdown-friendly drive-thru option seems years away. Plus, the thought of trying to eat liquor in my car terrifies me. Imagine smashing back a jellied eel while doing 70 mph on the dual carriageway. Eating jellied eels stationary is a big enough adventure.

She will kill me for this but I think it should be shared, as it is a feat of physics and determination. I have a vivid memory of my mum eating jellied eels in a La-Z-Boy reclining chair and placing the eel bones on the arm of the chair on a piece of kitchen roll. The feelings that image stirred in me were a mixture of disgust and astonishment. How could something so unseemly be performed so casually and with such grace?

Big Suze's approach to life will always amaze me. She has so much confidence in her convictions. She gave me a piece of advice which has always stuck with me. It has really helped me in my career and personal life whenever I have been nervous or my confidence has wavered. The advice was 'just because the *situation* changes, it doesn't mean *you* have to'. It's so simple yet effective. I remember when I started getting more TV presenting jobs and I was worried that I was too working class and raw. I used to second guess what the producers would want me to wear or how I should act. I even thought about trying to soften my accent to fit in. But my mum's advice was spot on. The producers had chosen me because of who I am, a funny-looking little blond bloke from South East London with an accent and a big gob. They knew what they were getting. Even if I did change who I am and it got me more work, it would be a terrible way to earn a living. I can't think of anything worse than being on a hit TV show that ran for years and years but having to put on an act every day. There is something so pure and thrilling about being totally yourself every day of your life. I would happily work less and be myself than work every day but pretend to be someone else. So that wise old seafood-eating owl has guided me through a number of challenging work days with that jelly-covered nugget of gold. So whenever you see me on telly, I am metaphorically reclining in a La-Z-Boy and eating jellied eels, not caring about what anyone thinks of me.

So my kids aren't keen on the food of my forefathers, but they do love McDonald's – or, as they call it, 'Chip and Burger'. My firstborn called it Chip and Burger when she was really young and it has become part of the Beckett family vocabulary. Even now, if me and Lou are hungry after a night in the pub and the kids aren't with us, I will refer to the Golden Arches as Chip and Burger, much to the amusement of our friends and, on occasions, the cab driver.

Growing up, I never trusted children who had never had a McDonald's. Certain middle-class parents absolutely love telling other parents that their kid has never had a McDonald's. It's said with the same level of smug pride as their child graduating from university or buying their first home. In my experience the kids who are banned from food and drink as kids go mad for it as adults.

Lou was not allowed fizzy drinks as a kid. Her mum used to dilute fresh orange juice with water. How hardcore middle class is that? Not diluted orange squash, but actual real-life orange juice from a real-life orange diluted with water. But in spite of this Lou has become a Diet Coke fiend. She smashes through the stuff as if it's the only liquid she's allowed after eating 20 bags of ready salted Walkers crisps. When we first started living together I couldn't believe how much she got through. She would buy 48 cans on the big shop to put in a cupboard.

I, on the other hand, don't really have fizzy drinks at all. As kids we were allowed fizzy drinks at Christmas, birthdays and special occasions. That was enough to get a taste of the good stuff without becoming addicted or resenting it being outlawed. I'm not saying let your kids have whatever they want, but if you ban them from it completely then I think it creates a bigger monster. We did, however, have lots of alleged 'freshly squeezed' orange and apple juice in cartons as kids. We thought they were healthy and good for you, but they were crammed full of sugar. I remember one summer holidays when I had about two litres a day of Sunny Delight until it got banned because it started turning people's skin orange. I was furious because it was delicious and I thought I was getting a great tan. Plus, everyone in South East London and Essex is orange anyway. A little top-up from your drink can't hurt.

I did have a bit of a KFC problem as an adult, on a level with my wife's Diet Coke issue. I had KFC once as a kid in Woolwich in 1997 as a treat after a trip to the dentist. Which, as you can imagine with teeth my size, was quite the ordeal. We started using a horse vet in the end because he had access to the appropriate-sized tools. I had a chicken burger and chips, and I loved it. It was like I was tasting America. This burger had been cooked by a colonel from Kentucky. I have always found the thought of America so sexy and exciting. I have been to the States a number of times and still get that boyhood excitement, like I'm in a real-life Hollywood movie.

As much as I enjoyed my burger, it didn't matter, as my mum couldn't taste America. All she could taste was gristle in her dodgy bit of chicken and she declared it the worst fast-food restaurant chain in the country. In my mum's defence the bit of chicken she had did look horrendous. All parents have a habit of not liking something, therefore their kids never eat it again until adulthood. Kidney beans are on that list at the Beckett family table. My mum hates kidney beans with a passion. To be fair, she's been on a dialysis machine for 20 years, which might create an unconscious bias. That's a joke. As far as I'm aware my mum has perfect kidneys. My dad, however, is *sans* spleen due to it being removed because of a precancerous tumour that didn't fully turn into cancer, thankfully. We found that out after a week of worry. Life is hard, isn't it?

Anyway, back to the Colonel. My mum still calls it Kentucky Chicken, totally refusing to jump on the KFC rebrand. KFC is also quite expensive for fast food, so whenever we did want fried chicken my mum could use the 'Kentucky chicken is too expensive' excuse. Which was totally fair, as the chip shop on Kimmeridge Road in Mottingham did six wings and chips for 99p. Even the Colonel himself couldn't argue with that.

So to me, as a child, KFC was an aspirational brand. I still vividly remember when I started to gig more regularly and earn more money, and I had a realisation that if I wanted to I could afford to eat KFC every day for lunch. And what's more, it turned out that I did want to eat KFC every day for lunch. I could so I did. I ate KFC for lunch every single day for three weeks, slowly working my way through the menu. It's not going to be a surprise to you when I tell you what happened. I put on weight, lots of weight, very quickly. But was I happy? Boy, I was over the moon. I was nailing life. I was eating KFC every day and I could afford it. I eventually calmed myself down and spread out my KFC lunches throughout the year – special treats and so on. I now save KFC for hangovers and wakes.

When you've grown up working class but end up working in a middle-class world, the kind of work friends you socialise with changes dramatically. Jimmy Carr loves to throw parties at his house for a wide-ranging group of friends from his private life and working life. Now, let's make it very clear: Jimmy has parties at his house. He does not have 'house parties'. They are two very different things. Working-class people have house parties. Middle- and upper-class people have parties at their house.

A house party is when you and your friends go to the off licence, grab some booze and take it to a person's house to drink. Sometimes you don't even know the person whose house it is. You have been given a street name and you walk down that street until you hear music. There will be loads of people squeezed into a three-bed terraced house, all rammed into the kitchen and spilling out into the garden. If you have brought premium lager or spirits you will hide them somewhere in the kitchen or keep them in the blue offie bag between your legs so no one can steal your drinks. If you have brought shit lager you will put it on the kitchen side then hunt out better-quality drinks.

I remember, as a teenager, trying to find house parties before we had mobile phones. We would just have a street name and a town. I would leave my house with 'Marsala Road, Lewisham' written on a piece of paper. The old trick would be to go into a petrol station to look up the street name in an *A–Z* street atlas. This makes me sound like I was born in the 1950s, but this was only 2002. When the internet really started to kick off we would print off Google Maps to take with us, like the Duke of Edinburgh's Award. It's weird being a millennial because you can use all of the new technology but you still remember VHS, MiniDiscs and mad cow disease.

There was always the rumour of a fight happening at a South East London house party. There was always a hard kid in the corner with all the girls, and gossip would circulate that another hard kid was coming down later with his cousins for a fight. It gave the whole event a real edge of danger and atmosphere. I do not agree with violence and I am definitely not a fighter, but I am a big fan of watching a fair fight from a safe distance.

The first time I got properly drunk was at a house party for a school friend's fifteenth birthday. It was a pour-your-own-drink buffet set-up. The parents had got a load of booze and laid it out on the table for us to help ourselves. As a 15-year-old boy I thought, *What a great idea and what wonderful, generous parents.* Now, as a 35-year-old father, I can't believe these mad fuckers were allowed to be responsible for children.

I got completely battered on gin and fresh orange juice. What a horrifically deadly combo that turned out to be. I got dropped home by a friend's dad. I knocked on the front door and my mum answered. She said I stood there swaying side to side with my eyes rolling in the back of my head, urinating on the doorstep. She stripped me to my pants and put me to bed, where I was sick in the night. My poor 13-year-old brother sharing the bedroom with me – he probably needs some sort of counselling, I must have looked possessed.

My drink choice shows how immature I was. I decided on gin and fresh orange juice because of Snoop Dogg. In the Snoop Doggy Dogg song 'Gin and Juice', Mr Dogg proclaims to be 'sippin' on gin and juice, laid back, with my mind on my money and my money on my mind'. I listened to those lyrics and thought, *That's a bit of me.* After being sick in the graveyard of the church next to the house party I did wonder if Snoop would drink ten double gin and juices with only a tube of Pringles to line his stomach. Truth be told, I was only 15 so I didn't have money on my mind like Snoop. I had exams on my mind because I had a Maths GCSE on Monday morning. I was hoping one of the questions would be 'on a scale of 1 to

10 how bad would Robert feel if he drank ten gin and juices with only one tube of Pringles?' The answer to that would be 10 and I had my piss- and sick-stained clothes to show my workings.

My chequered history at house parties did not adequately prepare me for a Jimmy Carr party. I was invited to a Mexican Cinco de Mayo party at Jimmy's house, so I got the Tube up there and popped into the off licence near his house. I bought eight cans of Heineken for me to drink and a bottle of Tequila as a present for Jimmy, secretly hoping that he would open it when I was there so I could drink it. I went for what I thought was premium special-occasion tequila, the gold colour label Jose Cuervo tequila. At this point in my life this was a huge treat, as normally I would buy the cheap tequila that had a coloured sombrero for a lid. For me, it was a special occasion, as I was going to a famous person's house for a party. I had only been on telly about three times so I was buzzing.

So I was walking along the back streets of North London, which always makes me nervous, clutching my bright blue off-licence bag full of beer and £20 tequila. Then the map on my phone told me that I had arrived at his house. It looked like a boutique hotel. The house was massive and beautiful and there was security at the front gates. I nervously said, 'I'm here for the house party.' I gave them my name and they let me in. Someone offered to take my bag for me but I panicked and said no. I walked into the main area of the house. It was such a big house that I couldn't even work out which room you would even attempt to call the front room.

I found the kitchen that opened out onto the garden and I saw about 200 famous people. This was the most random collection of famous people you will ever see. It was like a *News of the World* journalist's voicemail inbox. In front of me there were Elton John, Princess Beatrice, Kourtney Kardashian and, believe it or not, Anthea Turner. It was like I'd been transported into another dimension, and I was standing in the middle of it all, holding a blue bag full of Heineken and my special occasion tequila. I was well and truly a fish out of water. Never had my working-class roots been so obvious. My blue plastic bag was like a beacon of difference. I might as well have dressed up as a Pearly King and sung 'Knees Up Mother Brown' on arrival.

This party was mad. There were street food stalls in the garden serving tacos. There were waiters and waitresses serving drinks. I obviously looked scared and lost because a waitress found me and asked if I wanted her to help me find Jimmy. Eventually we tracked him down in another room that had a full bar like you would find in a hotel. He was standing there chatting with Russell Howard and Jonathan Ross. They saw me, then saw the bright blue off-licence bag, and all three of them absolutely ripped the piss out of me. It was brutal – a full banter assassination from three of the funniest men in the country. I vividly remember Jonathan Ross shouting,

'He's only been to the offy and bought his own fack-ing beer!' It was all good natured, fully deserved and very funny. If I was in their position I would have been doing exactly the same. But I was getting annihilated. Eventually I bit back and highlighted how mental this party was and that he should have warned me. I thought I was going to a normal house party, not some sort of hacking-scandal-victim meet-up.

The funniest part was when I gave Jimmy the bottle of special occasion Tequila, I then looked round and saw that he had about 50 bottles of it stocked up in his bar. Jimmy still had the class to thank me and mean it. He is a wonderful host and he made sure he introduced me to everyone so I didn't feel left out or alone. In the end I made a thing of the blue bag and carried it around with me all night. It made a good talking point, plus I was still working from my mum's logic that 'just because the situation changes, it doesn't mean you have to'.

When Jonathan and Jimmy wandered off it was just me and Russell left chatting. Russell was drinking a strong and whacky tequila cocktail that the waiting staff had been giving out. Then out of nowhere he asked me for one of my Heinekens. I couldn't believe the cheek of him. He had been rinsing me about my blue bag of beers for the last ten minutes. I said, 'Leave it out, mate. You were giving me banter about having them.'

'Oh, please,' he said. 'I hate tequila. I was only drinking it to be polite.'

I shared out my beers and relaxed into things after a pretty bumpy start. The party was absolutely brilliant, and Jimmy has a great skill in making sure an eclectic group of people all gel. I'm not exaggerating about this, the random people at this party was mind-blowing. Even Stephen fucking Hawking was there! I tried to talk to him but his friend said he couldn't talk because the battery was low on his machine. I smelled bullshit on that one. Who doesn't take a spare charger to a house party? Especially when it's his only way to communicate. In hindsight I was so shitfaced that I think I would have needed his computer to speak more than he did. I was drinking out of nerves, and at one point I was so pissed I walked straight into his glass patio door. There was actually an outline of my face on the glass, like a pigeon had flown into it. I might have been in a new unknown world but, for better or worse, I definitely made an impression.

CONFIDENCE

I truly believe that confidence is learned. No one is born confident. I think confidence is dependent on how your brain functions and what you have experienced in your life. I have not read or studied anything to back this up. This is just what I think from my experiences. If you want references and scientific evidence you need another book. I think people are born with different levels of chemicals in their brain which affect levels of anxiety and stress and depression. The levels of these chemicals will make it easier or harder to learn to become confident, but you still have to learn. I totally reject the idea that some people are born confident.

I was incredibly shy and anxious as a child, and to a certain degree I am still a shy and anxious adult, which is at odds with my upbringing, as my parents are incredibly confident. My parents operate in a manner that is oblivious to the opinions of other people, which in some ways is inspiring, as they will do whatever they want without fear of judgement or failure. But it can put you in awkward situations and conversations. I have benefited from this approach of attacking things carefree. My wife and friends call it 'being a Beckett' or 'that's going full Beckett' – where whatever is in front of you, your mental approach is, *I can sort this out*, and, *I can work this in my favour.* For example, if the sink is broken, my mum will invite her friend and husband over for a dinner party. It just so happens that the friend's husband is a plumber. Before you know it, between starter and main, the husband is on his hands and knees in the toilet fixing the sink. Simply a lucky 'coincidence'.

This, I believe, comes from their working-class backgrounds, where you have to do whatever you can to survive and get on in life. It's all a system of light-hearted banter and quid pro quo. Everything is stacked against you financially and socially, so you have to do whatever you can to climb the ladder and get by. My mum's argument would be, 'Yeah, he did fix the sink, but I did him a lovely chicken and leek pie.' Then cut to a few months later, when my dad or one of us boys is dropping off the plumber and his family at the airport because we owe them a favour. It's a working-class merry-go-round of non-financial repayments. Once, they had a bloke living in the spare room rent-free while he installed their kitchen. He needed somewhere to live for a few weeks and they needed a kitchen installed. Once the kitchen was finished he left. That never struck me as a traditional approach. I'm not sure they offer that service at Magnet.

Both my parents grew up without very much at all and have done incredibly well for themselves. Even though there wasn't loads of money and opportunities for me and my brothers growing up, compared to my parents' upbringing we had it easy. We were like little princes living the life of Riley. I imagine they had the same thoughts about their kids living different lives to them as I have about my daughters. So when I feel uncomfortable about an activity I'm doing with my kids because it's too middle class and boujie, imagine what it's like for my parents, who are another step removed. For them it's completely alien. They just can't compute why someone would book in these hipster baby classes. For example, when my eldest child was about four months old my wife booked us in for a baby massage course. The class was on a Wednesday afternoon and we had just got the baby to sleep. Fifteen minutes later Lou said, 'Right, we've got to wake the baby up, as we are going to be late for the baby massage class.'

I said, 'What are you talking about? It's taken an hour to get her to sleep.'

Lou replied earnestly with, 'We've got to go. Massage is really good for babies, as it helps them relax.'

I bit back with, 'She's asleep. How fucking relaxed do you want this baby to be?' Which unfortunately woke the baby up, suggesting that our baby needed to be more relaxed.

I told my dad about it and he wasn't impressed. 'I don't like it,' he said. 'Some stranger rubbing your baby with oil, giving it a massage. Where are you when they are doing it? In the waiting room?'

In my dad's head we had packed the four-month-old off on her own to Champneys for the weekend. She'd be sitting on a tiny lounger in a tiny robe, drinking a tiny fruit juice and waiting for her tiny treatment. I went on to explain that it was a class where the instructor teaches you where and how to massage a baby, and the parents in the class then massage their own babies with these techniques. It's not a spa retreat for tiny babies and no parents.

My mum is a big fan of a spa weekend with 'the girls'. I don't know why she calls them 'the girls'. There are six of them with the combined age of 403. They are definitely women. The spa weekend normally comes before one of my mum's health kicks. It's a unique approach to start a new healthier lifestyle. What they like to do is check in to the spa, have a swim, sauna, steam room and some treatments. They have a very healthy, low-carb and low-calorie lunch from the buffet provided. I'm talking boiled eggs, nuts and green pasta with no sauce – that kind of set-up. Then, after this day of disciplined wellness, they will all retire to whoever's is the biggest hotel room and proceed to drink 15 bottles of Prosecco between them. When they get hungry they wait for someone to sober up enough to do a McDonald's run. Unfortunately they are too drunk and their phones are too Androidy to order on Deliveroo. More often than not it's actually the giant, flappy leather phone case on Mum's phone that stops them from being able to access their apps when half-cut on bubbles. Either way, it sounds a lot more fun that ordering a salad on room service and sticking to the diet.

My parents get very comfortable very quickly. When I was in Australia filming the word count's best friend *I'm a Celebrity … Get Me Out of Here! Now!*, I flew my parents out for their birthday present and they stayed with me in the hotel. Weirdly, they have the same birthday, 9 July, but ten years apart. My dad is ten years older than my mum. I know, disgusting isn't it/I know, what a legend (delete as appropriate).

They met when they were 19. When my mum was 19, not my dad. That would be horrific and a matter for the police. While they were in Oz celebrating my dad still being alive despite the odds being stacked against him, as a special treat I took them to the jungle, where the show is filmed, and gave them a tour around the set. They got to meet everyone: Ant and Dec, Joe Swash, Laura Whitmore and whichever campmate had been recently voted off. I think they got to meet Limahl from Kajagoogoo, which was a bit anti-climactic for them after speaking to Joe Swash, who they love more than me. Which I totally understand. Joe has got to be one of the most caring and loving people I have ever met. As well as being one of the most naturally funny people I have worked with, he is also, in my opinion, extremely clever and more intelligent than he lets on. Let's face it, there is currency in being the silly working-class kid who gets stuff wrong.

I know, as in the past I have dabbled in that world. Sometimes truthfully – I still don't know how to pronounce quinoa – and sometimes I have stretched the truth for comic effect. With Joe there is an expectation from the media of what Joe Swash should be, and he plays his part perfectly. I know Joe Swash professionally as the cheeky chappy London boy done good. Super-loveable, a bit of a silly arse, just stumbling his way through life. I know Joe personally as an incredible dad and stepdad who has worked solidly in the entertainment industry for 20 years. A very astute individual who has enjoyed an excellent lifestyle for him and his family in that time. A silly arse just stumbling through life can't sustain that level of success.

Joey Essex is in a similar category. A working-class bloke from Essex, he's almost seen as a professional idiot. He will turn up on TV shows and give them the Joey Essex character. Now, I am not saying that Joey is a secret academic, but again he is incredibly switched on and successful and has been for years. But by playing up to these roles are we exacerbating the working-class stereotype? I don't think so. I think people like me, Joe Swash and Joey Essex come from quite sheltered environments and have learned about life on the job in front of millions of people on TV.

When I first appeared on *Mock the Week* I genuinely didn't know anything about politics. It wasn't an act to look ill-informed or stupid. I was ill-informed. As I have grown older in the last ten years, I have also learned a lot through life experiences, so I'm not the same kid who genuinely thought Austerity was the surname of a French politician. I know now that it's a government word for charging the public for the banks' mistakes. I think we should be expected to grow and learn as we get older. It isn't a sign of changing class or denying your roots; it's just what happens over time as you experience life. People do naturally change. I would like to apologise to Joe Swash and Joey Essex if I have blown your cover as the puppeteers and not the puppets.

As well as brushing shoulders with the stars and Limahl from Kajagoogoo, Mum and Dad were also allowed on the famous bridges the campmates use when they are voted off the show. As an extra-special treat Ant and Dec allowed them on the studio floor next to the cameras to watch the live show be filmed and broadcast to 13 million people back home in the UK. Now, for most people this would be quite a daunting and intimidating world. Not for Big Suze and Super Dave, as they showed during one of the commercial breaks.

As Ant and Dec finished the first part of the show, my mum, with a confident swagger reminiscent of the UFC fighter Conor 'Notorious' McGregor, walked across camera onto the set. Now, walking across the camera is a huge no-no in telly, and an even huger no-no on a live TV set. And an even more huger no-no when that live TV set is for the biggest TV show in the country hosted by the biggest stars on television. I stood there mortified.

I couldn't believe what I was seeing. It was like an anxiety dream. It's the equivalent of being an intern on your first day in an office job and your parents come to work with you and kick down the CEO's door during a board meeting because they fancy a chat. This was my first job in television – was I witnessing the beginning of the end of my career?

There were gasps from the crew. This was a two-minute advert break, when Ant and Dec practise their lines for the next part and make notes on their cue cards with the producers. Sometimes in those two minutes they will film extra parts of the show to be broadcast later as live. They might even use those two minutes to dash off to the toilet for a quick wee, all the while knowing that this urination was against the clock, as 13 million people are at home waiting for them. But today they did not have that option, as now they were the guests on a new show called *An Impromptu Chat with Sue Beckett*.

My mum strutted over and, in her defence, was very polite. She said, 'Ant and Dec, are you finished with these cue cards? If so, can I get your autographs, please?'

This was bad. Really bad. I contemplated stripping naked and jumping off the bridge head-first into the jungle, screaming, 'Stars for camp!' in order to create a distraction. Luckily, Ant and Dec are two of the friendliest and warmest people I have met in TV. They are also incredible at their jobs and nothing can put them off. They were not bothered at all – they just laughed at my mum's nerve and signed their autographs. My Mum said thank you and went back behind the camera. I was so lucky that it was Ant and Dec my mum did that to, as there are some other people in television who would not have reacted so nicely. Both Ant and Dec have working-class backgrounds, and I think they understood that my mum wasn't being rude – she was just oblivious to what was going on. I can imagine their friends and family might have acted in similar ways in their careers.

Worrying about other people's opinions can stop you from getting things sorted and progressing. So 'Being a Beckett' has its advantages, as my mum and dad have never been cowed by circumstance. This approach has really helped me with certain parts of my confidence. When jokes don't work on a TV show I have a Beckett resilience to plough on. Weirdly, the biggest threat to my self-confidence has never been external pressure. It's always been internal pressure, from the expectations I set myself and how harshly I judge my performance when I reflect on it. However, as well as the positives, 'being more Beckett' can spill over into, 'Let's do what's best for us whatever the situation.'

The first time Lou experienced my parents 'going full Beckett' was in Alicante airport. She is still scarred by the experience and it is in her top five drunk in-law rants. Every couple have a few anecdotes up their sleeve about the behaviour of their in-laws. Let me set the scene: Me and Lou were on holiday with my mum and dad in

Murcia. I was offered some work so I flew back early. But we couldn't really afford another flight for Lou to come back early, so she stayed with them in Spain for a couple more days. Which is enough to be left with your in-laws in a foreign country. When it was time to head home, they got to the airport and were faced with a huge 300-person queue at the Monarch Airlines check-in desk. Remember, this is Alicante Airport, the main terminal for visitors to Benidorm in the middle of summer. The patrons in line for the desk are a cross between a *Shameless* open audition and a Millwall away-game coach-queue. This is where I hand over to Lou, as it's her story to tell …

I need to preface this by saying that I love my in-laws dearly; however, I also think they have no idea just how much middle-class panic they induce in me sometimes when they're going what's called 'full Beckett'. Not just regular Beckett, which is an experience that took some getting used to anyway, but FULL Beckett.

Regular levels of Beckett were already a lot. I'm not exaggerating when I say that I don't think every member of my entire extended family put together has ever made as much noise as just five members of the Beckett family at the first Christmas I went to. I was, and still am, entirely unequipped to deal with the levels of Beckett-ness that happen sometimes.

CONFIDENCE

At the start of our relationship I had so many drinks I wasn't thirsty for or food that I wasn't only not hungry for, but I actually really don't like, because I don't know how to say no to things in case I seem rude. So that's the groundwork we're working from here. Me, will do things I don't want to do so as not to be rude; them, would never think you were being rude if you said no, but also unlikely to take no for an answer.

So Rob's left this story in the airport, but before we've even arrived at the airport I'm already at record levels of stress, even for me. On our way to the airport Dave is determined not to put any more petrol in the hire car, absolutely determined that we can make it on what definitely looks like an empty tank. I have no other means of getting to the airport and really, really do not want to break down somewhere in the Spanish countryside while Super Dave redoes his mileage calculations. I offered to pay for some extra petrol to make sure we'd definitely have enough, but it's not the money, it's the principle. Dave is not putting petrol in that car.

To be fair to him, we made it and it was fine – but I didn't have a single peaceful minute for that entire journey, as I was obsessively watching the fuel marker hovering over empty for the hour-long drive, listening for every little noise from the engine or grinding of the car that might be the start of us rolling to a halt in the middle of a motorway.

So this was the backdrop to arriving at the airport. I'm not going to lie, after a couple of days out there by myself and then the car journey of potential doom, I was quite looking forward to having a couple of hours on the flight to myself. Sue and Dave had booked the extra-legroom seats and I was sitting further back in the plane. We were flying home with Monarch, which I think might have shut down by now, and it's not that much of a surprise when I think about the airport that day. It was the height of summer, so the airport was full and our flight was full. This was the main flight home from that area of Spain, and a lot of our fellow fliers were coming back from Benidorm. They were all English and most of them weren't the shy and retiring type.

Monarch had a whole row of check-in desks but only one open, and the priority customer check-in desk had a small sign on it saying 'Closed'. Now, to be clear, Sue and Dave weren't priority customers, but what they did have were two expired priority-customer cards.

Seeing the queue for check-in snaking around the airport, Sue and Dave decided to go 'full Beckett' on this and wait in front of the priority desk, completely ignoring the fact that it was shut and they weren't priority customers. I, on the other hand, did not have a card, expired or otherwise, so I just said I'd join the normal queue, three or four hundred people back, and see them in the departure lounge, as our tickets were separate anyway.

I joined the queue at the back while Sue determinedly waved someone down to the priority desk. I was watching this from a nice, safe distance now. It was not making me anxious, as no one knew I was with them any more, so I thought, *Good luck to them. Try that priority queue if you want. Show them your expired cards.*

I watched the confused man from Monarch direct them to the normal check-in desk, as the priority desk was shut, which I and I think most normal people would take to mean join the back of the normal desk queue. But no. Of course not. They just moved sideways from the priority queue to the front of the normal queue. At which point two things happened. Firstly, people from all along the massive queue started shouting at them about pushing in. And secondly, Dave walked up to me near the back of the ever-growing queue and, clearly thinking he was being very kind, took my suitcase and wheeled it determinedly off towards Sue at the front of the queue, as, 'You don't want to wait in all that – we're priority members.'

Now, to give them their due, neither of them were phased in the slightest by the entire planeload of Benidorm holidaymakers now shouting at them about pushing in. Sue merely responded with a very breezy, 'But we're priority members,' and turned back around towards the check-in desk. Which wasn't even the slightest bit true, as their cards were very, very expired. All three of us were now at the front of the queue while a whole plane plotted our deaths and shouted at us.

Before you say it, I did try to stay at the back of the queue, but Dave had kidnapped my luggage and taken it with him to the front. I made a quick decision that it probably wasn't going to be brilliant for family relations if I wrestled my 70-year-old father-in-law for a suitcase in the middle of an airport.

There's part of this I kind of have to admire; to have the absolute balls to effectively push in a queue in front of an entire planeload of people and then front it out and not be bothered in the slightest is impressive. They would have made incredible spies behind enemy lines. Literally nothing phases them. They just didn't give a single fig about what people might have thought about them, and that kind of confidence is incredible. I, on the other hand, was an absolute wreck. I couldn't look at anyone, I was bright red, all I could hear were people shouting at us. If I could have fallen down a hole and died in Alicante Airport, I think I would have done. All I wanted to do was check in and get on the flight as quickly as possible because my seat was separate to theirs and people might forget I was with them by the time the plane took off.

Sadly, this plan was also thwarted because Dave, being kind and thoughtful, didn't think I had any euros with me so bought me a drink on the plane and brought it back to me, at which point I was caught between being polite and saying thank you for my drink, and fighting the urge to hiss at him, 'Go away! People have forgotten I was with you and I don't want people to see you talking to me.'

It's Rob again, by the way. First things first, RIP Monarch Airlines. When Lou arrived home from the airport after her flight and told me this story, I was nearly sick with laughter. She had to have a brandy and a sit down. She looked like she had just come back from a tour of Iraq. Never has a story summed up my parents and my middle-class wife so well. I can still imagine the panic in Lou's eyes when my dad escorted her to the front of the queue. It makes me laugh every time.

My parents have a strange type of confidence that doesn't come from privilege. It's more of an 'Ah, fuck it, we've got nothing to lose' type of confidence. Which I think I benefited from when I first started comedy. That nothing-to-lose confidence was a godsend, something people born into privilege and a successful family don't necessarily have access to. If my dad was Billy Connolly or Dave Allen, I wouldn't have had the pleasure of the 'Ah, fuck it, I've got nothing to lose' mentality. I would have had an 'Ah, fuck, my dad is a comedy legend – I've got everything to lose' mentality.

What's great about parents is that whatever class you come from, they will always have an innate superpower to embarrass their kids and son- and daughter-in-laws. I can only imagine how annoying and embarrassing I will be to my children. They are only young and I've already done full drag and had a tube shoved up my arse on TV. God only knows what the future holds. Just to be clear, the arse tube and drag were two separate episodes. But if there is a TV producer out there who wants to combine the two then I'm your guy. Fuck it, I've got nothing to lose.

As a kid I was very shy and didn't have my parents' confidence. However, I am and have always been an attention seeker. You may think shyness and attention seeking are mutually exclusive, but I disagree. You can still be shy and an attention seeker. I've always wanted to perform and enjoyed the attention, but what stopped me was a lack of confidence that brought on my shyness, as I was anxious that I would do it badly. I was obsessed with doing everything perfectly as a child. But perfect is impossible so I ended up never trying.

The first time I ever went on stage to perform was when I was 23, to do my first ever stand-up gig. My opening line was, 'Fuck me, those lights are bright.' It got a laugh – by accident, I should add. I don't know why we use 'I should add' at the end of sentences. Surely it's unnecessary, as you have already added it to the sentence. Why do you need to tell everyone you 'should' do it? It's already been added. Forgetting that for a moment and back to my first gig, I was and still am astonished by how bright the stage lights are.

I believe class and education have a direct impact on your confidence. As I said earlier, in my experience people who went to a private school have so much more self-confidence than state-school kids. With a private education, as well as a focus on grades there is also more pastoral care. The classes are smaller and it's often easier to spot a child suffering with shyness and anxiety. There will be more opportunity for that child to receive one-on-one help to improve their confidence. There is also pressure on the school and teachers from the parents, who want value for money. They are paying thousands of pounds a year for their child to receive more time and energy. In a comprehensive class of 30 children, a shy and anxious child can often get lost in the crowd and the teacher might miss the warning signs. This is not a dig at comprehensive school teachers. It's the system and how society is managed that lets down state schools, not the individuals involved.

My wife is an excellent teacher. She is extremely passionate and has always been marked as outstanding in school and in Ofsted inspections. She has worked at some of the toughest schools in South East London and she would attempt to teach history to huge classes that would include children who came from poverty, were involved in gangs and came from homes where education wasn't a priority because of other external factors. How can you attempt to teach kids who are already caught up in crime and/or come from unsupportive family homes?

I had great teachers at my comprehensive school. They were excellent at their job and passionate, and their hearts were in the right place. But it's so much harder to offer one-on-one support when you have 30 kids and no teaching assistant. Especially at my school, where I would be happy to come home without having been in a fight. At no point was I aware that I was supposed to be getting an education. Once, some kids came up to the school to fight the hardest kid in my year, and they chased him across the football pitches on a motorbike while wielding a metal chain. It was like something from *Mad Max*. I didn't come home from school frustrated that I wasn't learning enough or getting enough attention. I was buzzing that three lads on dirt bikes weren't trying to assassinate me between biology and French.

When it comes to confidence in comedy, I have seen comedians who went to public school have a terrible time on stage for 20 minutes but be oblivious to how badly it's going. I've seen comedians from council estates be brilliant for 20 minutes and come off stage thinking it went terribly. I'm not saying there aren't middle-class people who are shy and anxious. But they are more likely to have a confidence skillset that was moulded and created in school. Some of the most seemingly confident people I have met in the entertainment business are, deep down, insecure. Confidence is all bollocks and bluster – it's a cover-up. People mistake confident people for people who are happy and relaxed. Confidence is not a by-product of being content and happy. It is a learned skill to appear care-free and happy. I think it must be easier to develop your confidence at a young age if you are given more time and attention from parents and teachers.

As a person I've learned to become fairly confident, but as a performer I have bulletproof confidence. Put me on any show with anyone in the world and I will hold my own. I don't know how or why, but I can access that level of confidence in the moment. But that confidence evaporates as soon as I leave the stage or studio. The nagging voices kick in, because I am a shy, anxious person who has learned to be confident.

I still can't watch myself back on screen. I can't do it. All I see are flaws and imperfections. Sometimes I'm at home in my jogging bottoms and a baggy T-shirt, flicking through the channels, and I will come across myself on a TV show repeat. I'm watching myself but it's like looking at a different person. I can't believe I did that, and that confident person is me. Even in the moment it's like an out-of-body experience. I look down at myself, like I'm possessed, and the shy and anxious Rob has no control.

A CLASS ACT

As I watch myself on the screen, I'm lying on the sofa and working up the courage to take the bins out, while my confident alter-ego is somehow peeling a banana with his feet on *The Jonathan Ross Show* in front of Priscilla Presley and Elvis Costello. So, in karate terms, as a person I am a yellow belt in self-confidence. But as a performer I am a full black belt. Hopefully over time, as I grow as a person, I can become as confident off-screen as I am on it.

POVERTY MINDSET

I have a confession to make. I have, for five years, told my dad that I do my own garden. The truth is that I have a gardener and I don't have any equipment. I don't even own a lawn mower. The problem is that my gardener is excellent and my grass is always the most beautiful green colour; it is lush and thick with zero brown patches. My dad always asks me what grass seed and fertiliser I use, and I always say just the Homebase own-brand. So, Dad, you will just have to ask the gardener because I have no idea. I'm sorry I have lied to you for this long. It makes me cringe that I don't do my own garden. I have two young kids and I spend a lot of the time travelling and am away from home. It makes sense to have someone take care of the garden. I have no idea about gardens. I might be able to save some money if I did it myself, but it would take me about 12 hours and it would still look shit.

I had no idea what a poverty mindset was until I was told I had it. First of all, I want to make it clear that I have never lived in poverty or anything close to it. That would be completely unfair on my family and the people who have to endure genuine poverty. Poverty mindset is a broad term for an idea about how some people approach life and money, which is dependent on their upbringing and mentality. A poverty mindset is when you believe that you will never have enough money so you should never spend your money, as the opportunities to earn more are limited. Basically, if you grow up skint, as soon as you can earn money you work as much as possible to earn as much as possible, because you believe the money tap will be switched off at some point and there's no safety net to catch you. It perfectly collaborates with imposter syndrome, which is when you don't think you belong in an industry or believe yourself to be as competent as others think you are. You feel like you are blagging it and someone is going to tap you on the shoulder and tell you to get out of the club.

For me, the combination of poverty mindset and imposter syndrome led me to burnout. I felt I had to work harder than anyone else to maintain my position and get the financial security I craved. My greatest fear was all my work stopping and becoming a failure. It would begin a spiral in my mind: if I wasn't perfect and the most committed, I would lose work, then I would lose my home because I had no money, then Lou would leave me because I was a loser. This would carry on and escalate in my mind until I was on the streets alone. Obviously this is all ridiculous, but in my mind it felt so real, so I tried to work longer and harder than anyone else.

One of the only people in comedy that I think worked as much as I did was Romesh Ranganathan. I used to use Romesh as a benchmark and think, *I need to work harder than him.* But the problem was that we were both motivated by the same poverty mindset and imposter syndrome, so we just spurred each other on to keep working like maniacs. I think that motivation brought us closer together. He's one of my best friends and it's so helpful to have him to talk to about these things. We both have the same mindset, come from working-class backgrounds and don't feel we belong sometimes. I was so happy we hosted the *Royal Variety Performance* together. I enjoyed it so much more than I would have done alone.

I still think it's incredible what Romesh has achieved as a first-generation immigrant. His parents arrived in the UK from Sri Lanka in the 1970s and their son was the first person of colour to host the *Royal Variety Performance*. What an achievement. But what is more remarkable is that when I am out and about with Romesh and young Asian kids come up to him and ask for photos, I can see how important he is to a generation of children. When I was a kid, I swear that Sanjay and Gita in *EastEnders* were the only Asian people on TV. So now to see Romesh as one of the funniest comedians and best broadcasters in the country, it makes me proud to be his friend and, as much as he resists it, his double-act partner.

So, for ten years in the entertainment industry, because of my poverty 'it's all going to go tits up soon so cash in' mindset, I said yes to almost every single thing that was offered to me. Luckily, I have a brilliant manager, Danny Julian, who is excellent at guiding me away from bad decisions. I nearly did the celebrity diving show *Splash* back in the day, which I would have been terrible at. I don't like heights, I'm not a strong swimmer and I've got a body like a bag of mashed potatoes. But if it wasn't for Danny, I would have been diving into that swimming pool before you could say, 'What's the fee?'

The thing that stopped me from always saying yes and complete burnout was Covid and the first lockdown, when it was illegal for me to work and I had to stay at home for months. That's right, the only thing that stopped me from working was that my job was illegal. When lockdown first started, I was in the middle of a sold-out UK tour that was suddenly postponed for a year. My greatest fear had happened, there was no work and I had no income. But the reality was that it gave me time to rest and relax and rethink my approach. The thought of something is always worse than the reality. I have suffered from anxiety throughout my life, and I build things up in my head and get nervous and worried if there's something big coming up. But I am always okay in the moment, and in some cases I excel, as the anxiety is gone by the time the event I was getting worked up about is actually happening.

When the worst did happen and all my work was cancelled, my life didn't fall apart. It gave me time to rest and recuperate from a 10-year obsession motivated by fear. I started to be kind to myself and not keep beating myself with the fear stick. I also started a podcast with Josh Widdicombe about parenting, which has become one of the most fun and successful jobs I have ever had. It also enabled me to work from home and earn money in a different way.

I never thought it was possible to earn money without it being physically exhausting. For years I have associated success and hard work with being exhausted at the end of every day. Even with stand-up comedy, which is almost more of a hobby than a job, I transformed it into a physical and mental challenge. I couldn't just do a couple of gigs in London a week and chill out. I vowed to work harder than everyone else on the circuit. Ever since my first ever gig in 2009 I made sure I did at least four shows a week. For the first three years of that period I was also working in a full-time job. I used to sleep on the floor of the disabled toilet from 5.30 to 7.30 p.m. in between my office job ending and my comedy gigs in the evening. I got a sick sense of pride out of it, almost like battle scars to show how committed I was. I stuck to that promise of four shows a week for 11 years. The thing that stopped it was a pandemic that shut down the world. Looking back, it was madness, but it was the only way I thought you could be successful. The truth is that it's better to work smarter, not harder. But you couldn't tell me that at the start of my career.

Even now, I still find myself being controlled by my poverty mindset. Just the other day I was building some Lego. I love Lego. I find it very calming and therapeutic. I like being told exactly what to do and when to do it, which is one of the reasons why I am happily married. I was building *The Simpsons* House and I was doing it really quickly. When I realised how fast I was completing it my mind went into panic mode. I started thinking, *I should slow down, as the fun will be over soon and I can't afford any more Lego. I'll have to wait until Christmas or get some birthday money.* It was like my childhood mind had woken up from a coma in a 35-year-old man's body.

The truth is that, without being Billy Big Bollocks the Bad Boy Brigadier of Bragging, I'm a grown man and I can buy as much Lego as I want. Apart from the Millennium Falcon, which is £650. I don't care if I win the lottery, that one is getting left on the shelf out of principle. But the point is, why am I getting worried about finishing a Lego set too quickly? The reality is that I have two small children and I never get much chance to do my Lego. It's the time I am short of, rather than the money.

I have still got the Lego *Ghostbusters* House in the loft, unopened, which I got as a thirtieth birthday present. It's a big build and I haven't had the time to do it. Considering I've been in three lockdowns during that time, I'm not going to get the chance to build that *Ghostbusters* house until my kids leave for university. By then the unopened Ghostbusters house will have become extremely rare and valuable, so I won't want to open it, as it will be a waste of money.

My problem is that my brain is still living in the past. It still thinks of me as a scared kid who doesn't have much disposable income, any kind of career or confidence in his ability. My brain ignores all the stuff that is currently happening because it decided on who I am years ago and hasn't accepted that I have grown and developed. I am like an iPhone 12 that is still using the original iPhone's operating system. I have all these capabilities and opportunities, but I can't access them or see them because I'm trapped in an old way of thinking. I still function, but with the mentality of a scared child rather than that of a 35-year-old self-sufficient man. My challenge going forward is to push away those thoughts and really focus on the truth of who I have become – not what my brain decided on 20 years ago.

My poverty mindset kicked in again when I was asked to write this book. I didn't have a laptop or computer. I just thought I would use Lou's. But then we had to use the laptop for home schooling, so I had nothing to use to write my book. I kept telling myself that it was a waste of money to buy another laptop when we already had one in the house. *I will just write the book after 3 p.m. when home school finishes*, I thought.

Let's be honest, home schooling most days was finished by about 10.30 a.m. Some days, home schooling never even started. One day, my children just watched all 57 episodes of their favourite TV show *Bluey*, which is about a cartoon dog from Australia. We put that lesson down as geography. Even with an early home-schooling finish, sharing a computer with your wife and two children who all need to use it is an insane decision.

Eventually, I convinced myself it was sensible to buy a computer to write my book. I mean, surely writing a book is the best reason anyone could have to buy a computer. But for me I still had to convince myself that I wasn't being wasteful. Looking back now, I find it hilarious that I ever worried about it. But my brain, with its old operating software, kept telling me, *You can't buy a brand-new computer. It's too expensive. It's not for people like you. Get a second-hand one, or a discount or a deal. You can't just go to the Apple website and buy a computer – are you mad?*

It seems like crazy talk, but at the time it did feel like I was being really flash. I still remember when I first started to get on the telly and my brother Dan called me a 'flash bastard' when we were in Sainsbury's. We were getting a meal deal each for lunch. However, I went rogue and paid extra for a bottle of Ribena rather than sticking to the meal-deal drink options. Looking back, I think he might have been a bit early with the 'flash bastard' shout. In fact, Ribena is now included in the £3 meal deal so maybe I was a visionary.

I constantly worry about how my actions will be perceived, always have. I am desperate to be the same 'normal' bloke from South East London. But the reality is that all people change over time and you shouldn't be ashamed to change too. The key thing I need to do is ensure that I download the latest software in my brain so I can operate to my full potential and actually enjoy my life rather than worry all the time. I need to remove the outdated opinions of myself from my mind, so that I can relax and enjoy the world and life I have created without panic or self-judgement. Because if I don't sort that out then I'm just a grown man crying because he's building Lego too quickly. As I carry on writing this book, the more I worry it won't get released. I will just be sectioned, and this will be used as evidence. I just hope that other people have similar thoughts about themselves and can relate.

When I first started to do comedy, I was trapped in an office job I hated. I started off as an administrator on £17,500 a year. The job was boring, but the social side was incredible. I was working for an events company based in Camden. They would organise and deliver huge company conferences and parties all over the world for big organisations. I'm talking mega-billion-pound companies like IBM, RBS and GSK. You know it's a mega company when they shorten it to three letters.

Because we were organising events for the big dogs it meant that every single five-star hotel and top-end restaurant wanted us to use them for the events. When these hotel reps looked at me, they didn't see a skint chancer from South East London. They saw a skint chancer from South East London who had access to million-pound event budgets. So they would invite employees of the events company to their venues for 'familiarisation trips'. We would be given free food and drink so we could 'familiarise' ourselves with what our clients would experience if we picked their venue for the event. This wasn't any old food and drink – it was top-level canapés and champagne.

I learned so much about how rich people live during that time. My mates from work used to take the piss out of me because I had to google the menu whenever we went anywhere posh. We were invited to enjoy a tasting menu at Alain Ducasse at the Dorchester, and it was like the menu was in hieroglyphics. There was so much French on the menu I had to use Google Translate in the end. Over a couple of years in that job my palate expanded exponentially. I tried foie gras, oysters, yakitori and cocktails. I had never really had cocktails before, unless you count a jug of Woo Woo from Wetherspoons as a cocktail. Personally, I never have, and I never will trust a cocktail served in a jug.

I did make a few faux pas in my time (I learned 'faux pas' on a familiarisation trip too). I'll be honest, I still don't really know what a jus is. It's just a bit of sauce, innit? Once, I was being shown an events space at a hotel, and when we sat down to talk about the ballroom I started eating what I thought were vegetable crisps. It was, in fact, potpourri, which is dried petals and spices used to perfume a room (for those who don't know what potpourri is, because a 22-year-old me had no idea). I can't tell you how long I have spent on Google trying to work out how to spell potpourri. I'm still not sure I've spelled it properly.

I don't know if anyone reading has ever eaten potpourri before, but it's the weirdest sensation I have ever experienced. My mouth instantly went on fire, but not from spice. It was a fire of floral. It was the most confused and disgusted my mouth has ever been. It was like someone had put a rose garden in a blender and then I'd necked a pint of it. Even weeks after, I would be sitting watching the telly and would feel something in my teeth. I would wiggle it out and then, again, my mouth would fill with the taste and smell of the high-street soap-shop Lush.

My party trick on these trips would be 'one popping' food. As you may or may not know, I have a very large mouth, and I would show off when drunk and attempt to get food that usually takes a few bites down in one go. In one pop, if you will. Something like a donut, a burger or a full family trifle. Normally at fancy events the guests are offered canapés, which are designed to be eaten quickly and easily in one go. Then there is 'bowl food', which is a bigger version of a canapé in a bowl with a piece of cutlery, designed to eat in a few mouthfuls. But for a drunk 22-year-old attention-seeking Bobby Bigmouth Beckles, who hadn't found his outlet of comedy yet, it was an opportunity to shine.

I would be passed food from all over the room to 'one pop' for a laugh. Sometimes one after the other, for the full effect. I ate nine mini-burgers in a row once, purely for attention. Another time, I drank two bottles of free champagne and one-popped five bowls of olives for attention. I hadn't eaten anything else all day, and when I went home I was obviously violently sick. I will never forget how frothy and green it was. It came out of me like a wave from the sea. I remember thinking to myself, *I don't think anyone else in the world has done what I have done*. It was almost like a science experiment. What would happen if in one day you only had two bottles of champagne and over 50 green olives? Well, I can tell you what would happen. No need to give it a go, Professor Brian Cox. What happens is your mouth does a Jolly Green Giant frothy jizz explosion.

Some of these parties and events that we organised would cost millions. I say 'we', but I did sod all, apart from a bit of filing. There was no need for me to be on these 'fam trips', as I had no influence on which venue was picked for the event. Normally one of the senior people in the company would cancel last-minute due to childcare issues, then I would swoop in like a single, child-free vulture. I was like a pig in shit. I loved a fam trip. I used to do about five a week. Some weeks I wouldn't even go shopping. I would eat and drink in London hotels, pretending to look at event spaces.

However, this only lasts a couple of years, as you run out of venues and your body can't take the booze and rich canapés any more. I was so drunk over those two years. I just couldn't say no. The working-class part of my brain could not say no to free champagne. The debauchery and hedonism of that time actually helped me when I got into the entertainment industry, as I had got the partying out of my system by the age of 24. I could just focus on being a good comedian, as I had hit it hard already.

People sometimes say that comedy is the new rock and roll. That is complete bollocks. Comedy is full of nerds and people who never fit in growing up. It's really well behaved, in my experience. Office work is the new rock and roll. They are a bunch of animals. My time working in an office with a load of 20-year-olds pissed up in hotels, pretending to care about meeting rooms was way more reckless and out of control than comedy. I used to go to the pub at lunch for an hour and have four pints. That's ridiculous behaviour – how did I get any admin done? But maybe it was just my age or because I didn't love what I was doing. It won't come as a surprise to you that during the 2008 recession I was made redundant. But the company were very kind to me and found me another admin job, in the accounts department. I found this position even more dull and it stopped me from going on fam trips, as everyone knows that the accounts department don't choose the venues.

In that time, with my job prospects looking bleak, I started to do stand-up. I loved it so much and that's when I set myself the four gigs a week minimum goal. This was four nights a week gigging, by the way. If I did four gigs in one night I still had to find gigs on the three other nights that week. I used to turn up at open-mic shows that I wasn't even booked to be on and beg for stage time. There's a tiny pub called the Queen's Head on Denman St in the West End. It had open-mic nights on every evening, seven days a week. Once, I turned up and begged to go on and the promoter said he had no space on the bill. I kept on at him and in the end he said I could do a one-minute set at 10.30 p.m., before the end of the show. This was at 6 p.m. and he must have thought I would turn him down and go home. I accepted his offer and did a one-minute set at the end of the night.

I was obsessed with getting better at comedy. It was a mad period but I was driven by passion and excitement, so it was easier to keep up with my schedule. The gigging made me calm down my drinking, as I was working 40 hours a week in the office and four gigs a week in the evenings. Sometimes London, sometimes Nottingham or Bournemouth – or wherever and whoever would have me. These were all unpaid gigs and I had to pay for my own transport. I remember once being dropped off at Vauxhall bus station at 1 a.m. after a gig on the south coast. I was waiting for a night bus to take me back to Lewisham, knowing I had to be at work at 8 a.m. in Camden. But I didn't care because I had so much passion for what I was doing.

Back then my poverty mindset was my greatest asset. It powered me through. If I hadn't had that mindset I would never have made it as a professional comedian. Which is why I have a love-hate relationship with my poverty mindset. When used positively it can be so powerful. I become focused, relentless and so much more committed to my goals. But it's not sustainable.

I became a machine. I wasn't really enjoying or experiencing anything; I just had a numb focus that would get me through the day. Then, at the end of the day, I would crash at home on the sofa. I became a human doing, not a human being. I was never able to live in the moment and enjoy what I was doing, as I was driven by fear and would always be planning what my next move was. I never had time to stop and take it all in, as stopping to congratulate myself was a weakness that would stop me from reaching my goals. I was addicted to progression. I would ignore what I had achieved and move on. I would think it couldn't be taken away from me if I was still working. Resting on my laurels and getting caught lacking petrified me.

This approach brought me a few achievements and some people's version of success. But this workhorse mentality led to some really low moments. If you are constantly working to exhaustion every single day over 12 years, solely driven by fear, there is only one outcome.

On 4 January 2021, I wrote the below about the previous year in my phone notes when I was on my own, in tears. I don't know why I was writing it down. This book hadn't been commissioned and I don't really post personal stuff on social media, but it came pouring out of me, unprompted.

A CLASS ACT

On 4 January 2020 I was nailing it. I had just
flown into Cape Town, South Africa, in first class
to film a TV show. I was booked business but due
to an admin error I got upgraded to first class
for free. Lucky me! The TV show was watching
cricket, drinking beer and going on safari with one
of my best mates AND getting paid. This filming
was squeezed in during a nationwide sell-out tour.
Happily married to the love of my life, with two kids
in a family home newly renovated, I had surpassed
my wildest dreams. But I was the unhappiest I have
ever been. I woke up on 5 Jan in a five-star hotel
room thinking it would be better and easier for
everyone if I was dead. I still can't tell you why I
felt like this. A combination of working too much
coupled with severe self-doubt and anxiety. I put on
a smile and finished filming. I got back to the UK
and told my wife and my friend/manager how I felt.
I went straight to a therapist who I saw weekly for
six months. I still check in with the therapist when
I feel the darkness creep in. I paid for this therapist
privately but ten years ago I went through the NHS
and it was just as effective. I am telling you this as I
always promote the message that people should talk
about mental health but I rarely do. So here I am
talking. I wanted to die when I had everything I ever
wanted. So never judge yourself for feeling low. Tell
someone and they will help you feel better.

What I have really learned is that a poverty mindset isn't a terrible thing on its own. What makes it problematic is the fuel being used to drive it. At the start of my comedy career I was fuelled by passion. As time progressed and my success, fame and responsibilities increased, I was driven by fear. Fear of it all going away. When I started I had nothing to lose. But in South Africa I had everything I'd ever wanted. It felt like there was only one way it was going to go from there.

The truth is that if I'd carried on working that hard it would all have fallen apart. But acknowledging that I was unhappy and doing something about it, along with having time off to recover and reflect, rejuvenated me. I realised that I could be as productive and still deliver on stage and on camera if I was motivated by passion, not fear. I realised that your job can be hard and high-pressure and you can enjoy that feeling. It doesn't have to be this brutal factory-floor grind, where in order to be successful you have to suffer. Of course things can go wrong. You might not reach your goals, you might not get the promotion or bonus, you might not win the match or the contract. But so what? What's the worst that can happen? Will it end up with you depressed in a hotel in Cape Town wanting to die? Because that's already happened, when I'd hit every target and reached every goal. So why don't we try it another way? As my mum would say, 'Try it. It might be your favourite.'

I am now motivated by excitement and possibilities, not the fear of losing it all. I no longer set targets based on what other people see as success. Who cares if you've sold out the Hammersmith Apollo and are flying first class if you're crying in your bed. I no longer live in fear of failing to reach society's idea of achievement. Each day can be a success if you go to bed after enjoying your day and you look forward to the next one. It has taken a long time and been quite a journey to get to this place, but I think Rob Beckett the person is learning to be as confident as Rob Beckett the performer. Now, isn't that a scary thought?

EPILOGUE

When my publisher suggested I write an epilogue, I said, 'Yeah, sure, that sounds like a great idea. I was thinking of doing that anyway.' I then hung up the phone and googled 'epilogue'. I then googled 'why do we still say "hung up" the phone when we've pressed a button on a mobile phone?' The answers are that with old phones you would physically hang the ear piece on the top of the phone dial; and an epilogue is a section at the end of a book that serves as a conclusion to what has just happened.

I think we all know what's just happened. I tried to write a book about quinoa and pie mash and it took a left turn and got a bit fucking heavy. I never set out intending this book to be so serious in places, but I think that's the exciting thing about writing a book, you never really know what's coming next. Or maybe that's just because I sat down with zero planning, just my loose neck and a dream.

I found myself starting to talk about one thing in particular and, before I knew what was happening, loads of memories would fall out of me. I think I had locked them away as a way of dealing with them. When I'm performing live I try to be as honest as I can on stage. But when there is pressure for a laugh every 20 seconds the honesty can get in the way of a punchline and it gets dropped. Writing a book meant I was sitting here alone with no pressure, so my true thoughts and feelings had the time and space to appear. I've never really had that before. And as it's not live, you can go back through the book and add lighter, funny anecdotes to balance out the heavy parts. I mean, what I am trying to say is that books are a great way to communicate. I really think they are going to catch on in a big way.

The main aim of this book was to work out what class I am now. Am I still working class or am I middle class now? Even after finishing writing the answer is still complicated. I think I was desperate for an easy answer so I could pick a side and crack on. Book a pheasant-shooting weekend or a trip to Wayne Lineker's Ocean Beach bar in Ibiza. I still don't know which class I am, but the most liberating thing I have discovered is that I don't really care any more.

I was oblivious about class when I was growing up. I just thought everyone was like me because I hadn't really experienced anything else. Then, as an adult, it was clear I came from a different background to my peers, but I didn't think about it too much, as I was distracted by my career. The only reason I started to really think about the impact of my class was when my kids came along. I felt

I needed to answer those questions in order to work out who I was and how to be a good dad to them. Having children really made me think about what was happening and whether I'd end up having anything in common with my two middle-class kids.

The truth is that I don't really care about class. All I care about is having the best relationship possible with my wife and children. Class and the privilege of opportunities and experience are the clear points of difference between me and my children. I thought that if I could pinpoint this class difference between us then I could try to narrow the gap and all my problems would be solved. But I was wrong. The truth is that they are going to live a different life to the one I've had, and that's great. It's a positive thing. That's the point of it all, isn't it? Making sure the next generation have an easier path. I have to accept that my 5-year-old child will correct my grammar and have a favourite artist at the age of 5, when I don't even have a favourite artist at 35. It's Yayoi Kusama, if you're interested. Nah, I had no idea either. She is Japanese and does yellow and black pumpkin paintings, apparently.

I think the Covid lockdowns were hugely beneficial for me, as all my work being cancelled gave me the time to focus on my mental health. My greatest fear was all my work and income being taken away from me, and then it actually happened. Twelve months of work disappeared in one Boris Johnson speech. My biggest anxiety came true, but it wasn't as bad as my brain had imagined. The reality is that it's never as bad as your brain imagines. Anxiety is like the world's biggest reverse catfish.

The world coming to a halt enabled me to slow down and focus on being in the moment a lot more. I stopped worrying about the past or panicking about the future. When I feel a relentless energy brewing and the negative voice in my head popping up, I now have a range of tools to calm down. I do colouring in, mindfulness meditation, Lego and seal clubbing. Not really seal clubbing – I stopped that years ago after a shoulder injury. Lou is such a brilliant wife and so understanding, and if she notices changes in my behaviour she will offer to take the kids out somewhere so I can try to calm my brain with one of these tools.

I also return the favour if Lou is ever feeling stressed and overwhelmed. Having that honest conversation with each other has been integral to our relationship. I remember once, before a summer holiday, asking her if she wanted to shave my back hair for me. She said, 'Do I *want* to shave your back? Absolutely fucking not. No, I don't *want* to shave your disgusting back hair but I will do it because you physically can't reach it.' She truly is the most wonderful mother and wife.

She has been my rock for the last ten years. We have a comfortable life now but when we first met and I was starting out in comedy she paid every bill and completely supported us financially for over three years on her teaching salary. I'm not going to lie, I have taken over the financial reins in the last few years and she's had an excellent return on her investment, but she was the one there at the start when I was skint and jobless. Something she likes to bring up and remind me about almost daily. Even more so when she wants to book a holiday or redecorate the house.

As I write this now, I feel the best I have ever felt mentally. Not by coincidence I'm also in the best physical shape I've ever been in. Don't get me wrong, that is not an impressive level of fitness. I spent my teenage years morbidly obese. I'm still a bit heavier than I would like but I'm making progress. I am now what you would call 'not fat stood up'. When I'm up and about I look half-decent. It's a very different story when I sit down – my belly expands over the elastic of my pants and my nipples face the floor, like a dog being told off. But standing up, I look all right, especially first thing in the morning. I am like a different person. Post morning poo, pre-breakfast, I can almost sit down topless in front of the mirror and not be physically disgusted by myself. As soon as I have a bacon roll and a coffee I put on two stone again.

I have lost ten pounds and I am enjoying exercise now. I feel more positive. When I was low I would train out of body shame and panic, and I hated every second of it. Now I am less harsh on myself. I enjoy the buzz I get after a workout. I'm no Joe Wicks. I've still got a hairy back and dad tits with chunky nips, but I've made a start. My plan is to get ripped at 40. I want to do a full Gary Barlow. He had a few heavy years in his thirties, then at 40 he was on *The X Factor* with a six-pack and a jawline you could use for a Pythagoras equation.

As well as exercising, I have slowed right down mentally and lightened my workload. I have actually started saying no to work for the first time since I started doing comedy. Apologies to *Strictly* and *I'm a Celebrity ... Get Me Out of Here!* I know my time will come to ruin my marriage and eat a crocodile's vagina on TV, but not just yet. Now that I have slowed down I have started to notice the seasons. I know, it sounds silly, but I was so busy in cars and theatres and on planes that I was never aware of what was happening around me. I had pure tunnel vision.

I discovered magnolia trees this spring. Now, that tree has got some serious swagger when it flowers. Big bastard petals out of nowhere for about three days. But, word of warning, when those big boy petals fall to the ground and they turn brown and sit rotting on the pavement like dog shit for weeks, it's like mother nature is trolling you. By the way, just because I notice flowers now, I don't want you to think I'm not still a fucking geezer. Sure, I notice the seasons, but I'll still drink ten pints of lager in a pub beer garden with a bucket hat on. And sure, I might complain about the price of a mature Japanese acer tree, but don't think I won't still do a Jägerbomb and go to an afters.

Now, I know what you're thinking: *Come on, Beckett. Shut up about magnolia trees, you chilled out hippy dickhead. Why don't you care about what class you are any more? I've read a whole fucking book about you working it out and now you don't care.*

Fair point, reader. This is why. At the moment my relationship with my kids is better than ever. I've stopped worrying about what my relationship will be like with them in the future or how far away from my experiences they'll go. Sounds too simple, surely? Like all the best things in life, simplicity is king. Worrying about your relationship with your kids is pointless, as it's driven by fear and anxiety. If you're worrying about the future you can't be in the moment. And if I'm not in the moment then I'm not actually experiencing the relationship with my kids. I'm caught in a purgatory of worrying about things I have done with them and the impact that it will have and worrying about what I'm going to do for them in the future and the impact that will have. When you are thinking about those things it stops you from being present in the moment with them.

The reality is that the best thing I can do for my children is be 100 per cent present in the moment and connected with them whenever I'm with them. That will have the most impact on your relationship, as being there is the best thing you can be for your kids. Being there is the only thing you can really do. When the chips are down and life comes at you hard, money and success won't solve your problems. All you want is your mum and dad to be there.

Of course, I don't want to be there for all of my kids' major life events. I'll take a pass when they go on a first date or lose their virginity. I think sometimes a parent can be there too much for their kids. But whenever they do need me they know that I'll be there for them 100 per cent, whenever and wherever. Rich or poor.

Ultimately, you can't make sure everything is perfect for your kids. The same way that you can't make everything perfect for yourself. You try your best and wish them luck. My relationship with my kids is way stronger when I'm in the moment with them, playing Yorkshire Pudding Catch, rather than worrying that they might not appreciate a holiday they haven't had yet because they are too middle class. Or worrying that saying the wrong thing in front of their school friends is going to scar them for life. You can't control the future and you can't change the past. The only thing you can affect is the now.

Ironically, I had this realisation when I was driving my kids to a toy shop. When we parked I got my phone out to write down my thoughts before they evaporated. My kids were in the back screaming about something while I wrote down how important it is to be present with children. Absolutely not practising what I was preaching, I panicked and jumped into action. I put the phone down and started to get them out of the car, and I became Captain Present Dad. Commander of the Moment. As I unclipped their car seats both my daughters started to cry because I was interrupting the game they had been playing. They'd been perfectly happy playing in the back while I wrote my notes, but my anxiety about not being a good-enough dad kicked in unnecessarily.

The truth is that kids are easy. It's us parents who overcomplicate it. That's what I have done, I've overcomplicated it. You don't need grand gestures with kids – they don't know or care what class they are or what they're doing. They couldn't give a shit. They are simple creatures. A child will lose their mind with excitement over a trip to Disney, but they will also lose their mind with excitement eating a packet of Hula Hoops while watching *Mamma Mia! Here We Go Again*. Which is absolute dog shit.

The first film is an absolute classic, though. My kids know all the words to the first one. If you've never seen a three-year-old do a live rendition of 'Super Trouper' you're missing out. They have been watching that film three times a week for the last year, and I only found out today that at one point Meryl Streep says the word 'slut'. That's some first-class parenting there. Working on three viewings of the film a week, if my maths is correct, my three-year-old has heard the word 'slut' 156 times from Meryl Streep alone. That's not ideal, is it?

Now that my kids are sorted, what about me? Does class matter to me when I'm on my own in those lonely, quiet moments you sometimes get no matter how many friends and family you have? When you catch yourself having a deep think out of nowhere? You're on the sofa having a scroll through social media and then, all of a sudden, you start to question who you are and what you have done. Am I a loser? Have I become a prick? Am I a good enough son? Am I enjoying my life? Why is my dick so small?

What I have realised writing this book is that I have had a severe case of imposter syndrome for almost my entire career. Not only with my class but also in my ability as a performer. I've never felt like I fit in, wherever I am. My mum's advice 'just because the situation changes, it doesn't mean you have to' has been imperative to me in my career. It enabled me to stick to my guns and not be manipulated by the industry. However, I stuck to the advice too rigidly and it held me back. It made me feel like I was behind enemy lines and I didn't deserve to be there. I was so paranoid about not fitting in at work but also changing too much to fit in at home that I've been stuck in a no man's land of class. The fact of the matter is that the advice isn't to never change. It's simply that you don't have to change. If you want to change or you end up changing that's okay too.

I have discovered that I am proud of my working-class roots. My mum and dad made huge leaps socially and economically in their lives, which their children have carried on and so will their grandchildren. They might not have got every decision right, the same way I won't get every decision right with my parenting. But the intent has always come from a place of love and support. It's all about family progression.

My parents have been on a different journey to me. They started with much less than I started with so had no time to process how they saw themselves. As I mentioned earlier, when you're trying to survive there's not time to think about how you could thrive. But the support they have given, along with Lou, has helped me develop to a point where I now do have the time to think about how I could thrive. Hopefully as the family progression continues my children won't ever give thriving a second thought. It will just be a part of their life.

What I've come to realise is that what I have changed isn't my class, it's my opinion of myself. I didn't realise how badly I thought of myself. I now know my own worth, and I don't think I did before, which is why I was so hung up on class. I thought looking outward at class would help me understand and process who I am and what was happening to me, both professionally and at home, raising kids who do ballet and go to baby massage. But it wasn't as simple as, 'Well, I was that class because I did this, and now I'm this class because I do that.' For years I beat myself up, telling myself I wasn't good enough or I wasn't working hard enough and that ultimately I didn't deserve to be there. I had no respect for myself. I was told I was never going to be a high-flyer and I believed it, so I treated myself like I was a loser. A loser who got a lucky break.

Whenever I was interviewed by journalists I would reel out the same old line when asked about my career. I didn't understand what was happening to me so I would always say 'comedy is just a hobby that got out of hand'. Whereas actually it wasn't a hobby; it was something I loved and had worked really hard at for 12 years, and I was good at it. But I found it easier to believe that it was me getting lucky rather than me being able to achieve something. Believing in yourself is the key to being content and happy. If you don't back yourself why would anyone else? Life is hard and full of enough people who will give you shit. Don't allow yourself to become one of those people.

I never envisaged this book ending with what feels like a load of self-help bollocks, but it looks like it has. Right, I'm off to celebrate finishing it with a bottle of champagne and a doner kebab. Why? Because I can. I'm classless. Right, you've had your twenty quid's worth out of this book. Now fuck off out of my business, you nosy bastard.

ACKNOWLEDGEMENTS

Lou, not only are you the love of my life and the most important person in the world to me, but without you this book wouldn't have been written. From your patience listening to me blabber on about it for months to sitting down, reading it and giving me notes. Thank you so much. My beautiful girls, you will never know how much joy you give me. There are no words to describe how much I love you. I am wrapped around your little fingers and I am happy to stay there forever.

Kelly Ellis, my publisher, your advice, guidance and calm persona have been invaluable. Thank you so much for taking a chance on me and giving me the opportunity to write this book. I hope you're happy with what I have produced, because let's face it, you took a leap of faith on this one.

Danny Julian, the best comedy agent/manager/friend anyone could ask for. I've never known someone who works so hard and cares so much about their acts. In a business full of wrong'uns, who knew the Millwall fan from a council estate in Bermondsey was going to be the most reliable and trustworthy person I would meet? Also, a big thank you to Joe Norris, Richard McCann, Ann Kennedy and everyone else at Off the Kerb.

A big thanks to Charlotte Brown, Sean Mahoney and Penny Boreham for their help with the audiobook – without you it wouldn't have happened. It got tough at times, so thank you so much.

Thank you, Ray Burmiston, Faye Sawyer, Liv Davey, Paul Sweeney and Manze pie-mash shop for the brilliant cover photo-shoot.

The Howats, you got a whole chapter, so this is all you're getting here.

Sue Winter and Daniel Constantinou, you both know why you are so important.

Thank you to Tom Allen for allowing me to bore you with my ideas for the book on our long walks in the woods and puddle jumping. Also a big shout-out to Phil Kerr, Lottie Brooksbank, Martin Wallace, Tom Packman, Lloyd Griffith, Kishore Nayar, Romesh Ranganathan, Josh Widdicombe, Tim Carey, Jack Greenaway, Chris Birch, Luke Thomas, Kenny Love, John Freeman, Philip Skinner, Luke Goody, Amanda Emery, Mick and Teresa Watts, Aunty Tina and my brothers Russ, Darren, Dan and Joe.

There are loads of people I have missed and I can apologise to you in person. Mum and Dad, I love you to pieces and let's be honest, I think you got off lightly.

PICTURE CREDITS

Plate-section images courtesy of the author, with the follow exceptions: p8 (top) Edward Moore; p9 Andy Hollingworth; p10 (top) Gary Lashmar; p10 (bottom) Philip Brown/Popperfoto/Getty Images; p12 (top) Brian J Ritchie/Hotsauce/Shutterstock; p12 (bottom) Nigel Wright/ITV/Shutterstock; p15 (top) Geoff Pugh/The Daily Telegraph/PA Images/Alamy Stock Photo; p15 (bottom) John Phillips/Stringer/Getty Images; p16 (top and bottom) Matt Frost/ITV/Shutterstock